PLAYS VOLUME 2

by the same author

NOVELS

NO ANSWER
THE INQUISITORY
MAHU OR THE MATERIAL
BAGA
SOMEONE   *in preparation*

PLAYS

THE OLD TUNE   (New Writers 2)
PLAYS VOLUME I   (Clope, The Dead Letter,
                  The Old Tune)

PLAYS
VOLUME 2

Architruc
About Mortin
The Hypothesis

ROBERT PINGET

Translated by Barbara Bray

 HILL AND WANG · NEW YORK

Architruc and *L'Hypothèse* originally published by Editions de Minuit, Paris, 1961
Autour de Mortin originally published by Editions de Minuit, Paris, 1965

Library of Congress catalog card number: 66-15897

First American edition 1968

Printed in Great Britain

CONTENTS

Architruc

CHARACTERS

THE KING
BAGA, *his minister*
THE COOK
DEATH

A mean room pretentiously furnished. Right, a bed with a canopy, an armchair, a table, a bearskin rug. Back centre, a door. Back left, a partition concealing a dressing-room, extreme left, a cupboard. In the middle of the room, a green plant in an ornamental pot.

When the curtain rises the king is seated in the armchair. His crown is on his head. He is wearing a dressing-gown. He inspects himself, adjusts his collar, scratches at a little mark on the lapel, dusts his sleeves, puts his feet into his slippers. Then he takes up a little mirror from the table, looks at himself, arranges his hair, puts his tongue out at himself. Grimaces. He puts down the mirror, picks up a pair of nail-scissors, and begins to cut his nails.

KING: *to* BAGA, *who is invisible behind the screen*] Ready?

VOICE OF BAGA: Not quite. Another minute.

KING: But what are you doing? We said we'd keep it simple. What are you dressing up as?

VOICE OF BAGA: An ambassador. Must make it true to life.

KING: True to life! Don't make me laugh, Baga.

BAGA: Belt up.

Pause. The KING *continues cutting his nails.* BAGA *hums a tune. The* KING *makes as if to get up.*

KING: I'm going to look.

BAGA: Looking's not allowed. I'm nearly ready.

Pause. BAGA *is heard pulling the chain.*

9

KING: Did you—?

VOICE OF BAGA: No—just a piece of cotton-wool.

KING: *shouting*] For the thousandth time, you're not supposed to put things down the lavatory! We've got the most colossal bills for having them unstopped.

VOICE OF BAGA: Sorry y'r majesty.

KING: Of course you don't have to pay for it.

VOICE OF BAGA: And I suppose you do? Always putting it on your subjects.

KING: You leave my subjects alone and come out of there.

VOICE OF BAGA: Just the finishing touch . . . there.

Longish pause. The KING *fidgets about with the things on the table.*

KING: Ready?

VOICE OF BAGA: Ready.

BAGA *appears dressed in a ridiculous sort of musketeer's get-up. Cloak, sword, plumed hat. False moustaches. Heavy make-up. He makes a ceremonious bow.*

BAGA: My humble duty, Sire.

KING: *acknowledging the salute without rising*] That's me. What can I do for you?

BAGA: You don't say what can I do for you, you say we are graciously pleased to hear you.

KING: We are graciously pleased to hear you.

BAGA: I must say it's a poor show when you haven't managed to learn the forms after all these years. You don't try.

KING: Oh hell, I thought we were supposed to be amusing ourselves. Go on.

BAGA: *repeating his bow*] Sire. You cannot be ignorant that my master the King of Novocordia has claims to the succession of your crown. The law introduced by your great-grandmother—

KING: You're not going to start that again, are you? Taking advantage of being dressed up? I forbid you to mention the subject.

BAGA: All right, all right. I'll start again. [*Bows again*] Sire. You cannot be ignorant—

KING: You might vary the words a bit.

BAGA: All right—you have a go.

KING: *He rises and bows, doffing his crown*] Sire. Your Majesty is fond of good cheer. Permit us to suggest a menu for this evening.

BAGA: Imagine an ambassador suggesting a menu!

KING: Why not? you can't go wrong with a menu. It puts people in the mood for generosity, fair play . . .

BAGA: And then what does he try to get out of you?

KING: My daughter's hand in marriage to his master.

BAGA: Good God!

KING: What, don't you like the idea?

BAGA: It's not that, but you'd have to beget a daughter first.

KING: Are we supposed to be acting or not?

BAGA: Yes, but we ought to keep the thing credible.

KING: Credible! You give me a pain.

BAGA: Oh, I do, do I? and supposing I did nothing but sleep, like you, who'd collect the taxes? The only thing you can do is spend all the money on food.

KING: I haven't got anything else to do. I can't rely on your conversation any more. [*Pause*] What have we got for dinner today?

BAGA: We said we were going to relax for an hour. What's decided is decided. I shall continue. [*Bows again*] Sire. You cannot be ignorant—

KING: What, again?

BAGA: —that my master wishes to marry. Rumour has it that your daughter is the most beautiful girl in all the lands you hold in fee—

KING: Heavens, that reminds me—I haven't watered Fifi. *He gets up, fetches a little watering-can from a corner, and goes and fills it in the dressing-room. Meanwhile* BAGA *sits down and thinks, making calculations on his fingers.*

KING: *coming out of the dressing-room with the watering-can and watering the plant*] Must never forget to water Fifi. She's a very rare plant—

BAGA: *reciting*]—that came to me from my Aunt Estelle, cost a thousand rupees, is of the female gender, has four hairy leaves and invisible sexual organs, is . . .

KING: Go on.

BAGA:—is very delicate and must be brought indoors in winter.

KING: Not that. The embassy.

BAGA: *getting up and bowing once more*] Sire. You cannot be ignorant that my—

KING: *banging the watering-can down on the table*] For heaven's sake! Think of something else.

BAGA: I haven't got any more ideas. You upset me. [*Pause*] Actually I think I preferred your mother.

KING: You used to sleep with her, I suppose?

BAGA: A bit. Nothing to write home about. But at least she left the initiative to me as far as the government was concerned. If your crown's still on your skull don't forget it's thanks to me.

KING: *seated again*] We don't want to hear all that.

BAGA: *striding up and down the room*] Naturally. I've unmasked conspiracies, you know. I was responsible for the conduct of the Chanchèze war. And I signed a commercial treaty.

KING: Your master-piece! Yes, do let's hear some more about that! We haven't got a crust left between us.

BAGA: People have to learn restraint. In the interests of higher things. [*Pause*] Anyway, you don't look so bad on it.

KING: Go on.

BAGA: You're as fat as a friar, you've put on five—

KING: Not that. The embassy.

BAGA: I told you I haven't got any more ideas.

KING: Then let's discuss the menu.

BAGA: No. I'll go and dress up as something else.

KING: If you keep chopping and changing the fun can't be expected to last.

BAGA: Nobody mentioned fun. It was recreation we were after. If you've got to have fun into the bargain . . .

KING: Sulking, eh, your excellency?

BAGA: You make me tired. It's about time—

KING: Oh, don't put yourself out.

BAGA: I'll go and dress up again.

KING: Go and dress up again then.

BAGA *goes back into the dressing-room. The* KING *doesn't know what to do with himself. He picks up a letter from the table, reads it under his breath, shows signs of impatience, puts it down again, picks up the mirror, puts that down again too. Long pause. Then he gets up and goes over to the dressing-room.*

KING: I'm going to look.

VOICE OF BAGA: No! It's a surprise.

KING: But what's it like?

BAGA: You'll see. Read your love-letter.

KING: It bores me. [*He turns back to the table. Bends down and strokes the bearskin rug.*] Poor old dad. He used to go bear-hunting. Domestic troubles. Was he as bored as I am? [*Pause*] What can he be up to? [*To* BAGA] What about going down to the kitchens? [*Pause*] Can I have a pernod?

VOICE OF BAGA: Strictly forbidden.

KING: Won't you let me just once? Just this once?

VOICE OF BAGA: Certainly not.

KING: Just for once while I'm waiting!

VOICE OF BAGA: Oh all right, just for once then. But only a little drop.

KING: Jolly good! [*He claps his hands. He goes over to the cupboard, opens it, takes out a bottle and a glass and carries them over to the table. Serves himself, using water from the watering can.*]

Do you want some?

VOICE OF BAGA: Later on.

KING: *sits. Drinks*] Mmm, that's the stuff. [*Raises his glass*] Do you remember when we were in Fantoine?

VOICE OF BAGA: What?

KING: When we were in Fantoine, the pernod parties we used to have! Shall we go back?

VOICE OF BAGA: It's not the holidays yet.

KING: Still we could treat ourselves to that.

VOICE OF BAGA: Government affairs first. Anyway, be quiet, I can't do two things at once.

KING: There's no need for you to answer. [*He goes on drinking. Stands up, slightly drunk, with his glass in his hand, and starts to act the part of the ambassador.*] Sire, your most

14

humble and obedient servant. [*Pause. To* BAGA.] Is that right? [*Pause*] I'm talking to you.

BAGA: Wrap up.

KING: *as before*] My respects to her highness your daughter. [*Laughs. Pause. To* BAGA.] Are you going to be an ambassador again? [*Pause*] I'm talking to you! [*Pause*] What sort of thing is it? A king? A horse? [*Pause*] Oh, I know. A cook. [*As he speaks he goes nearer to the dressing-room.*]

BAGA: You're not to look!

KING: You spend too much time hovering in the wings. I'm coming in when I've counted three. One . . . two . . .

BAGA *emerges. He is dressed as a woman, in the style of* 1900—*bustle, large hat with half-veil, boa, parasol. He minces about the room.*

KING: Jolly good! You look just like Aunt Estelle. [*He imitates* BAGA *and goes over and sits down.*]

BAGA: *woman's voice*] My dear boy, I absolutely adore your room! So tasteful, so friendly! And such comfort, my dear! Dressing-room and all. You've inherited my taste for luxury, Architruc.

KING: No but you know she hadn't got such a big belly as you.

BAGA: *as before*] Oh, I see you've still got my plant! I'm glad of that.

KING: Yes, aunt. We call her Fifi. I water her every day.

BAGA: Quite right, my boy. It came to me through a negro cousin of mine, now dead, poor soul. She left me this plant and her purse with five rupees in it. But . . . you knew her, perhaps?

KING: Yes, a chubby little thing.

BAGA: Not at all. A great gawk like a man.

KING: Oh yes. If you like.

BAGA: Now, my boy. Tell me about your government. Tell me about your prime minister, Baga.

KING: A proper bugger, aunt.

BAGA: Architruc! How dare you? To speak like that to me! Do you know I might have been your mother?

KING: How was that then?

BAGA: Your father loved me first. We were very intimate. He had to leave me to marry my elder sister. That great numskull—

KING: I forbid you to insult the memory of my mother.

BAGA: *still in female voice*] All right, all right. [*Pause*] But . . . where *is* Baga?

KING: Gone to see his aunt, aunt.

BAGA: Really? Very funny. I see your conversation's improving. [*Pause*] Well, the King of Novocordia . . .

KING: Baga! Did you hear what I said to you? [*Pause*] And how's my uncle, aunt?

BAGA: The Marquis is very, very tired. The burden of his estates is too much for him. I . . . But what's this I see? Pernod?

KING: *getting up, all eagerness*] Would you like some? I'll get you a glass [*He goes and gets a glass from the cupboard, fills it, and is about to replenish his own.*]

BAGA: *normal voice*] Careful!

KING: Only one! The last!

BAGA: *snatches the bottle out of his hands. Normal voice.*] It's no use. I'm not going to let you.

KING: All right then, I shan't play any more. [*Turns his back on* BAGA.]

BAGA: *normal voice*] Good. I wanted to talk to you about some of the profits we made out of Chanchèze.

KING: *turning round hastily*] Really? Ooh, tell me!

BAGA: *normal voice*] If you'll go on with the game.

KING: I will.

BAGA: *female voice again*] Tell me, my boy, what do you think of your prime minister?

KING: An excellent fellow, aunt. [BAGA *nods approval.*] I'm extremely fond of him. We get on excellently. [BAGA *nods approval.*] But he will persist in forbidding me to drink pernod. There's no sense in it.

BAGA: Really? He probably has some reason. Your liver, perhaps? No? Your kidneys, then? Yes, it must be your kidneys. We all get old, you know, Architruc, nothing to be done about it. [*Pause*] So you say he's an excellent prime minister?

KING: First-class. Tell me about the profits, Baga.

BAGA: *normal voice*] Later. [*Pause. He tries out various poses. Normal voice.*] Now I'm going to make advances. Let's go on. [*He goes over to the* KING *and starts to flirt with him. Female voice again.*] Oh, what a sweet little nose it used to have!

KING: Idiot!

BAGA: And what pretty little eyes! And what beautiful little biceps! [*Tickles him. The* KING *laughs.*]

KING: That'll do.

BAGA: And what lovely little thighs! [*Pause. Normal voice.*] Well, say something! *Do* something. [*He runs his hands over his bosom and hips. Female voice again.*] Come, my darling, I can't wait any longer. [*He gets hold of his arm and tries to drag him over to the bed.*]

KING: Ow, you're hurting me. And it isn't funny.

BAGA: *normal voice*] All right, all right.

KING: Tell me about those profits.

BAGA: I won't tell you anything.

KING: But you'll tell me if I'll play? Very well—but not at love!

BAGA: *normal voice*] Hark at the puritan talking! [*He looks at his watch.*] Right. We've still got half an hour. I'm going to dress up again.

KING: What as?

BAGA: God.

KING: Jesus!

BAGA: *going over to the dressing-room*] Wait till I'm ready and no cheating. [*Goes into the dressing-room.*]

KING: God the Father or God the Son?

VOICE OF BAGA: You'll see.

The KING *automatically picks up the letter from the table, reads it again, raises his head, scratches, shrugs his shoulders. Pause.*

KING: Government affairs first indeed! What government? Every man for himself. [*To* BAGA] Are you trying to make a fool of me?

VOICE OF BAGA: Me? Why?

KING: Government! What government?

VOICE OF BAGA: Your subjects, for heaven's sake.

KING: My subjects! Have you seen them?

VOICE OF BAGA: I smell them. That's enough.

KING: What do they smell like?

VOICE OF BAGA: Awful.

KING: And do they still pay up? [*Pause*] Fine thing this at our time of life. [*Pause*] Is it a large amount? [*To himself*]

Anyway, what could we do with a large amount if we had it? [*To* BAGA] Ready?

BAGA: Ready.

BAGA emerges, dressed as a judge. Very dignified. He frowns.

KING: What's this? Did you change your mind?

BAGA: It's the last judgment. I am the supreme judge who is about to pass sentence on you.

KING: Well I never. I thought it would be funnier than this.

BAGA: God's not there just to amuse you. He's there to sentence you to death. Kneel down.

KING: Why, if I'm condemned already!

BAGA: Because you have to do as you're told. On your knees.

KING: I'm tired. And anyway I don't like death sentences.

BAGA: You're hopeless.

KING: Perhaps. I don't want to play any more.

Knock at the door.

BAGA: Come in!

Enter cook, cap in hand.

COOK: Dinner is served, your Majesty.

KING: What? I haven't shaved!

COOK: Monsieur Baga said—

KING: Who gives the orders here?

BAGA: I told them to serve it when it was ready.

KING: And supposing I'm not ready?

BAGA: You could go without a shave for once.

KING: And what about protocol? What about government? [*Signs to cook to go.*] Go!

Exit cook.

KING: Fine thing, I must say! I'm not allowed to do anything now! The slave of my own servants! *They* give *me* orders!

BAGA: Take it easy. I'll go and fetch your shaving-mug.

KING: You'll go and fetch it when I tell you to.

BAGA: All right, all right.

KING: Go and fetch my shaving-mug.

BAGA *goes into the dressing-room. He comes out still dressed as a judge and puts the shaving tackle down on the table. The* KING, *sitting in the armchair, looks very tired.*

BAGA: Don't you feel well?

KING: Not very. I'd like to go to bed.

BAGA: Do you want me to send for the doctor?

KING: No. [*Pause*] I think it's my complaint again.

BAGA: That's all we needed.

KING: *musing*] Baga, do you believe in the government?

BAGA: Do I believe in the government? What's the matter with you?

KING: My complaint. [*Pause*] Why don't I abdicate? I could go and live in the country. I wouldn't have anything to do. These subjects complicate everything. Stinking wretches in their miserable holes. Have you seen them?

BAGA: I tell you I've smelt them—their money reeks.

KING: *nodding towards the corner of the room*] Do you remember when the bed was over there? I think I liked it better.

BAGA: *makes a gesture of resignation and sits on the bed*] All right, do your complaint.

KING: Yes, I think I liked it better. It was gayer.

BAGA: It was us that were gayer.

KING: Do you think so?

BAGA: It's such ages since we did anything. Not even a little war. We're just rusting away.

KING: Have we really changed so much? [*Pause*] Baga, I'd like to talk to you about my childhood.

BAGA: *in consternation*] Oh no, no, please!

KING: Yes, I want to. [*Pause.* BAGA *shrugs his shoulders.*] I don't know where to begin.

BAGA: At the beginning.

KING: *Pause. He meditates*] It's funny—they're all alike. [*Pause*] I'd like to tell you about mine, but not in the usual way. I'd like to do it differently, somehow. [*Pause*] I'd like . . . I'd like to talk to you about my soul.

BAGA: Jesus!

KING: Yes, that's it, talk to you about my soul . . . And about life.

BAGA: What life?

KING: Life . . . life.

BAGA: There's *your* life. The things you do, the things you've done, your government, your—

KING: Only that?

BAGA: What do you mean, only that?

KING: It's impossible. So I haven't really got a life?

BAGA: Well, do you think I have? I've got documents for you to sign and the privilege of drawing up the menu.

KING: Don't you enjoy it?

BAGA: I can't remember.

KING: Neither can I. [*Pause*] Sometimes I tell myself that one could change.

BAGA: Change what?

KING: I don't know . . . Put the bed back over there, have the armchairs re-covered . . .

BAGA: Those aren't real changes, you know, Archi.

KING: What are real changes then?

BAGA: I don't know . . . Journeys?

KING: *suddenly perking up*] Baga, that would be marvellous! We'll go on a journey!

Pierce Library
Eastern Oregon University
1410 L Avenue
La Grande, OR 97850

BAGA: Where to?

KING: It doesn't matter where to! We'll pack our cases, we'll wash down dad's old taxi and we'll go!

BAGA: But where, I'd like to know?

KING: Well . . . to Chanchèze, for example.

BAGA: Chanchèze? That valley full of rats? What do you expect anyone to do there?

KING: Well . . . Dualia?

BAGA: And get frozen to death? No thanks.

KING: Well . . . Oh, I know . . . We'll go to Estellouse. They've finished working on it, haven't they?

BAGA: I was there last week. The castle'll have to be done all over again. The ceilings have fallen in and the cellars are flooded.

KING: Already? But they must have just done it any old how. When did they finish? You didn't say anything to me?

BAGA: My poor fellow, they finished a century ago. It's had plenty of time to go mouldy again.

KING: A century! And I've forgotten that castle for a whole century!

BAGA: That's what I call forgetting. [*Pause. He gets up and helps the* KING.] Why don't you lie down—you'll feel better.

The KING *stretches out on the bed.* BAGA *covers him up then sits down in the armchair.*

KING: Do you remember when I used to ask you questions? [*Pause*] I'm talking to you.

BAGA: Mm?

KING: When I used to ask you questions about nature.

BAGA: Oh please, not that, I'd rather you talked to me about your childhood.

KING: I can't remember anything any more. [*Pause*] Nature—what's it for?

BAGA: To rule us.

KING: That again? The sea, the trees, the mountains? [*Pause*] I think just the opposite. Anyway what I say is . . . No, I remember I used to say I'd give all your landscapes for a room overlooking a courtyard. [*Pause*] Provided there was somebody in it.

BAGA: *indicating the room and its contents, including himself.*] Well . . .

KING: Not you, Baga . . . I mean . . .

BAGA: Don't bother, I understand.

KING: No, that isn't what I mean. What I mean is someone...

BAGA: Someone you love?

KING: You know very well I love you, Baga.

BAGA: Well then what?

KING: Nothing.

BAGA: A woman perhaps that you can make love to?

KING: I—

BAGA: Making love from morning till night in a room overlooking a courtyard? You don't think you'd be fed up with it after three days?

KING: All right, let's say a room with a balcony overlooking the sea.

BAGA: That gives you two days more. Then what?

KING: Perhaps that's what life is? What do you know about it?

BAGA: What do I know about it? I know that we've been fed up with each other for a hundred years.

KING: But we haven't made—

BAGA: That doesn't make the slightest difference.

KING: Do you think so?

BAGA: I'm sure of it. [*Pause*] You need to make changes—

KING: There, you see.

BAGA:—while you still believe in them. After that it's useless.

KING: *dreamily*] A room overlooking a courtyard . . .

BAGA: Supposing I told you I'd have liked to be prime minister?

KING: But that's what you are.

BAGA: You see what I mean?

KING: Oh you make me tired. [*Pause*] I'm tired, I'm not very well.

BAGA: Do you want to sleep?

KING: No thank you.

BAGA: Something to eat?

KING: No thank you.

BAGA: Would you like me to tell you a story?

KING: Do you know any?

BAGA: I'll try. [*Pause. He tries to think of something.*] Once upon a time God said to himself . . . No. [*Pause*] Once upon a time there was a king and a prime minister.

KING: I see your game.

BAGA: Don't interrupt. [*Pause*] The king didn't know what to do, and neither did the prime minister. They racked their brains, but they couldn't think of anything. Then God said to himself, I must do something for these people. So he racks his brains, and he can't think of anything either. So he calls his counsellor, the serpent. And he says, do you see that king and his minister? Well, I want to give them some ideas. Think of something. So the serpent—

KING: Why a serpent?

BAGA: Don't interrupt. The serpent goes and gets his bag and brings it to God. There you are, he says, go on. What am I supposed to do? says God. Take something out of the bag. Anything? Yes, the first thing you get hold of. So God dives his hand into the bag and brings out . . .

KING: Is this symbolical?

BAGA: —and brings out . . . Just a minute while I try to remember. [*Pause*] Oh yes. A child. And God says to the serpent, this king is unhappy because he's all alone and he's worried about the succession. This child is a good idea. I'll send him to him. It'll give him something to think about. And he tosses the child down to earth.

KING: Is it symbolical?

BAGA: The kid falls on to the king's bed and he wakes up and says what's this urchin doing here? His prime minister says, Sire, it's a gift from heaven and you must adopt him.

KING: What are you getting at?

BAGA: Don't interrupt. The king says all right, what shall we call him? The prime minister thinks a bit and then says, Sonny. We'll give him a sound middle-class education and he'll succeed you on the throne. The king is delighted, forgets all his worries, doesn't think about anything now but his son. The son grows up, becomes a person of distinction, is a comfort to his father in his old age, and makes him die happy.

KING: Charming. [*Pause*] So you advise me to get married?

BAGA: No.

KING: To beget a son then?

BAGA: No. They're nothing but trouble. But you could adopt one. I've been thinking about it for a long time. The succession—

KING: Where should we get him from?

BAGA: The orphanage.

KING: And what guarantee would there be that he wouldn't turn out a rascal?

BAGA: You've got to choose between that and the crown going to the King of Novocordia.

KING: Never! I prefer adoption. [*Pause*] But what's got into you all of a sudden? Are you afraid I'm going to pop off?

BAGA: No, I'm thinking of your good, of your peace of mind.

KING: And that you're bored with me and a son would give you something to think about.

BAGA: Exactly.

KING: You're unkind, Baga.

BAGA: I am a prime minister, sire.

KING: *Pause*] A son—the idea terrifies me. Bringing him up. [*Pause*] Wouldn't you like him to belong to you too? Just a little bit?

BAGA: I'll be his godfather. We'll give him a bed in here and put his little clothes in the cupboard. And I'll give him lessons in government.

KING: How old will he be?

BAGA: Seven. They don't wet the bed any more and they understand what you say to them.

KING: I bet you've already taken steps and said nothing about it.

BAGA: No, but it was on my mind. [*Pause*] If you feel better in the morning we'll go and buy one at the orphanage.

KING: How much does it cost?

BAGA: In the region of a thousand rupees. It depends.

KING: Have you got any money?

BAGA: We can draw on the coffers of the state.

KING: How much is there there?

BAGA *pulls a cash box out from under the bed. He rummages about in it, and counts.*

BAGA. A thousand . . . two thousand . . . three . . . five . . . Five thousand rupees.

KING: Incredible! We can rebuild Estellouse as well, it can be my summer residence. [*Pause*] Oh, I feel much better! Can I get up?

BAGA: No. Tomorrow.

KING: What can we do till then?

BAGA: Do? [*Pause*] We could rehearse.

KING: Rehearse what?

BAGA: You could rehearse the part of father. How will you tackle it?

KING: That's true.

BAGA: Yes, we'll rehearse. I'll be the son and you be the father.

KING: Adoptive.

BAGA: Adoptive. [*He gets up.*] Now. Pretend I'm just coming in from the garden. On my scooter. I come in and scoot round the room. [*He imitates a child on a scooter and goes round the room. In an inane infantile voice.*] Hallo daddy! I do like my new scooter!

KING: Oh, how lovely, who gave it to you?

BAGA: *child's voice*] You did. I'd have preferred a motorbike.

KING: A motorbike at your age? Don't be silly.

BAGA: *child's voice*] I'm not a little boy any more, dad. I'm seven.

KING: Do you think I had a motorbike when I was seven?

BAGA: Of course not. You were too much of a dope.

KING: Is that the way to talk to your father?

BAGA: *child's voice*] Will you give me a motorbike when I'm eight?

KING: Not till you're fifteen.

BAGA: I'll ask my godfather for one.

KING: Who is your godfather?

BAGA: *still child's voice*] You don't even remember! It's Baga.

KING: And what did he teach you today, this godfather of yours?

BAGA: *still scooting around*] Division.

KING: Oho! [*Pause*] What's seven divided by three?

BAGA: er . . . um . . . eight.

KING: No, no, no. It's two point three three three three.

BAGA: How many times?

KING: To infinity.

BAGA: That's impossible.

KING: What do you mean, impossible?

BAGA: Only God is infinite.

KING: But—

BAGA: *normal voice. Out of breath. He is still scooting round the room.*] Couldn't you tell me to stop? Doesn't it get on your nerves?

KING: Yes. Boy, stand still when I talk to you.

BAGA: *child's voice*] No, I'm on the *Tour de France.*

KING: Stand still, do you hear?

BAGA: No, I'm in the middle of a lap.

KING: Well, what do I say now?

BAGA: *normal voice*] You won't let me have any dessert.

KING: Boy, I won't let you have any dessert.

BAGA: *child's voice*] What are we having?

KING: Er . . . What are we having?

BAGA: *child's voice*] I don't know, I'm asking you.

KING: *I'm* asking *you*.

BAGA: *child's voice*] But daddy, I don't know!

KING: *You*, Baga, you blithering ass!

BAGA: *normal voice, but still scooting round*] And supposing I'm not there?

KING: What do you mean, not there?

BAGA: *normal voice*] Supposing I'm in the kitchen? What will you say to him then?

KING: Go to the kitchen and see.

BAGA: *normal voice*] There's a fine way to bring a child up!

KING: Well, what should I say?

BAGA: *normal voice*] You say, no dessert, understand?

KING: No dessert, understand?

BAGA: *child's voice. Still going round*] I don't like dessert anyway, daddy.

KING: In that case . . . Oh well bugger it.

BAGA: *child's voice*] Ooh, daddy said bugger it, daddy said bugger it!

KING: *yelling*] Baga, stop it!

BAGA: *coming to a halt, normal voice*] Deplorable performance. [*He is exhausted and collapses on to the bed.*]

KING: What ought I to have said? Are they all like that?

BAGA: All. You have to be tough with them.

KING: But what comes next after the dessert?

BAGA: That's enough for today.

KING: It's not my fault. Couldn't we have chosen one a bit quieter?

BAGA: You mean one without any go in him? You'd rather have just a limp rag?

KING: No but—

BAGA: Well it has to be either a real boy or a limp rag.

KING: But why couldn't we have a girl? They're supposed to be quieter, aren't they?

BAGA: And what about the Salic law?

KING: All we have to do is repeal it.

BAGA: Impossible.

KING: Baga, surely you could do a little thing like that for me.

BAGA: I tell you it's impossible. We shall have to have a boy.

KING: Oh, all right. [*Pause*] I feel sad, Baga. Everything we do is sad, this room is sad, life—

BAGA: You're not going to start that again, are you?

KING: My soul is sad.

BAGA: Here we go!

KING: We're just straining ourselves all the time for nothing. I used to say to myself that it would change, I used to think . . .[*Pause*] If one could just withdraw. But I don't even want that . . . The spring of life is *wanting* . . . sounds like a very profound pun, doesn't it? [*Pause*] The spring of death too. When you don't want to you die like a dog.

BAGA? Have you quite finished? You don't have to think about such things. And anyway I'm here, aren't I?

KING: Yes, you're here. [*Pause*] A long, long journey! Wouldn't you like to? Why wouldn't you like to?

BAGA: But of course I'd like to. Where to?

KING: No, don't ask that. We'll pack our cases and go tomorrow.

BAGA: All right, let's pack our cases.

KING: *beaming*] Ah! [*Pause*] Oh, I feel marvellous! [BAGA *drags a case out from under the bed. He opens it, then goes over to the cupboard.*]

BAGA: How many pairs of socks? Three? Four?

KING: Five! We've got a long way to go.

BAGA: Five pairs of pants then?

KING: And five shirts and five handkerchiefs! And the tweed suit and a cap. Just the thing for a holiday feeling. [*Pause*] Don't forget the muffler and the dark glasses. We'll travel incognito.

BAGA: This passion for incognito! Everyone recognises us anyway.

KING: Yes but it simplifies the etiquette.

BAGA: *going backwards and forwards from the cupboard to the case packing.*] What are we going to do with Fifi?

KING: Leave her in the kitchen. They'll water her.

BAGA: Aren't you afraid she might die?

KING: If she dies she dies.

BAGA: Well, you *have* changed.

KING: *swaggering*] You have to learn to *act*! [*Pause*] Don't forget my slippers. [*Pause*] Think! Tomorrow we'll be going to bed in a different room!

BAGA: Overlooking a courtyard perhaps.

KING: A different room, different walls, a different horizon! A wide, wide horizon, infinity!

BAGA: *still busy with the case*] And what are we going to say to the maids? Who's going to look after them? They'll have a rare old time.

KING: Good! Let them enjoy themselves!

BAGA: And what about the cash-box?

KING: We'll take it with us. [*Pause*] Baga.

BAGA: What?

KING: The future is never as horrible as one thinks.

BAGA: Are we taking the camera?

KING: The future! Wring its neck! Knock its block off!

BAGA: Aggressive too!

KING: Baga, we're going to turn over a new leaf.

BAGA: About time.

KING: Never too late. We're going to make up for lost time, we're going to live! We'll use up all the money in the cash-box! We'll set ourselves free, no more ties, no more government, no more anything! We'll just launch ourselves into the blue! Ah Baga, liberty!

BAGA: Don't get excited, old chap. [*Pause*]. Where did you put your sun-glasses?

KING: The sun! Stark naked in the sun! [*He picks up the little mirror beside him and looks at himself.*] Do I look terribly old?

BAGA: *taking the mirror out of his hand*] Never mind that; rest. You're over-exciting yourself.

Knock at the door.

BAGA: Come in!

Enter the cook, cap in hand.

COOK: I haven't come about lunch, sire.

KING: Pity. What then?

COOK: It's . . . I think it's . . . I mean . . .

KING: Well, what?

COOK: It's not someone who's actually here, sire . . . I think it's someone being announced . . .

KING: By whom?

COOK: A dispatch-rider.

KING: Dispatch-rider?

COOK: Yes, a cyclist.

KING: Is he still here?

COOK: No, he's gone again.

KING: What did he say?

COOK: Well, he said ... umm ... He said ...

KING: Well, spit it out!

COOK: I don't know, sire, I didn't understand.

KING: But come, come, cook, what did he talk about, more or less?

COOK: I ... I think he said something about a rather peculiar menu ... Something like that.

KING: Who for? Me?

COOK: I don't know, sire.

KING: But you ought to have kept him, asked him to explain! [*To* BAGA] What does this mean?

BAGA: I don't know. [*To* COOK] Is that all he said?

COOK: Yes, I think so ... No, he said lots of things, but I didn't understand.

BAGA: He didn't say where he'd come from? Or who he wanted? What made you think he's a messenger?

COOK: I don't know ... He said something ... about a peculiar menu ... and then he went.

The KING *signs to* BAGA *that the* COOK's *off his head.*

KING: Very good, cook, very good. You can go.

Exit COOK.

KING: Poor boy. Does he get enough to eat?

BAGA: He gets enough to drink, that's certain.

KING: At his age? Perhaps he's having an unhappy love affair?

BAGA: *shrugs his shoulders. Turns back to the case.*] As I was saying, the dark glasses. [*He notes it down in a little book.*] . . . and provisions.

KING: A cyclist? A peculiar menu? [*Pause*] Do you know the cook?

BAGA: Know him?

KING: Do you know about his love affairs?

BAGA: Since when have I been the concierge, sire?

KING: You're not going to stand there and tell me—

BAGA: No, I tell you—I don't know anything about the cook's troubles.

KING: That's wrong.

BAGA: Wrong? You're going ga-ga!

KING: I'm the father of my people, I ought to know them.

BAGA: Well, call him back and ask him his secret.

KING: What do you think I keep a prime minister for?

BAGA: *Oh* no. Other people's secrets, no . . . I empty your chamber-pot, that's as far as I'll go.

KING: Very well, very well. [*Pause*] What sort of provisions are we going to take?

BAGA: A peculiar menu.

KING: You're bloody annoying.

BAGA: I am a prime minister, sire.

The KING *lies down. He turns towards the wall.* BAGA *does up the case, takes the watering-can from the table and goes into the dressing-room. He comes out with the watering-can and waters the plant.*

KING: *without turning round*] What are you doing?

BAGA: Watering Fifi.

KING: That's nice of you. [*Turns round and sits up. Beaming.*] Baga.

34

BAGA: Yes?

KING: We're going away! Oh I do feel marvellous! [*Pause*] What about going on with the play? Just for a bit?

BAGA: You rest.

KING: I'll rest, but first you dress up again, just once.

BAGA: *shrugging his shoulders*] If you like . . .

KING: What as?

BAGA: It's a surprise. Lie down and wait. [*The* KING *lies down, face to the wall.*]

KING: You'll tell me when?

BAGA: Yes.

> BAGA *goes into the dressing-room. A longish pause. The* KING *doesn't stir. The door back-stage just opens. Enter* DEATH. *It is taller than* BAGA. *A skeleton wrapped in a shroud, carrying a scythe. It steals into the room. The floor creaks. The* KING *turns round.*

KING: *frightened*] You made me jump! [*Pause*] It's rather good, you know. You look much taller.

VOICE OF BAGA: What?

> DEATH *goes over to the bed. The* KING *is frightened, covers his face with his hands.*

KING: Baga! You're frightening me!

VOICE OF BAGA: Just a sec! What's the matter?

> DEATH *brings down the scythe.*

KING: *terrified*] Baga! Baga! No! No!

> DEATH *cleaves the air above the* KING *with the scythe. His arms fall. He is dead, mouth open.* DEATH *goes out swiftly through the door.*

VOICE OF BAGA: What's the matter? Did you see a spider? [*Pause*] Answer! [*Pause*] Right. Ready then? I'm coming.

Curtain

About Mortin

Whisperings

—What's he doing?
—I can't see very well. He's gone over to the right. Wait.
   [*Pause*] No, I can't see.
—Try a different position.
—That won't make any difference.
—Try.
   Pause
—No, I can't see anything.
   Pause
—What is there over on the right?
—The bed and the screen.
—And he's behind the screen?
—I don't know, he might be behind the bed.
—Isn't the bed up against the wall?
—The wall's further away.
—Perhaps he's gone back to bed?
—I can't see. [*Pause*] He's come back to the middle of the
   room. He's holding a book. He's opening it. He's put-
   ting it on the table.
   Pause
—Is he reading?
—No. He's just standing. Looking at the book.
—Is he still in his dressing-gown?
—He's going over to the window.
   Pause
—What's he doing?

—He's bowed his head. He's leaning his right cheek on his hand.

—Has he got tooth-ache? [*Pause*] Has he got tooth-ache?

—I don't think so. He's thinking.

—What can you see through the window?

—The house opposite.

—Is there anyone there?

—I can't see, he's in the way. [*Pause*] There's a string of washing hanging at one of the windows. Underwear.

—Women's?

—I can see a pair of pants.

—Nobody at the window?

—He's coming back to the table. He's putting on his glasses.

—Is there somebody at the window?

—No. Just the pants, a shirt, two pair of socks. He's sitting down. He's opening the book.

—And he's still in his dressing-gown?

Pause

—He's looking for something in the book. [*Pause*] A post-card. He's reading it. He's looking up. He's taking off his glasses. He's looking at the card.

—Can you see what it's of?

—I can see some blue.

—And he's still in his dressing-gown?

—He's going to put it . . . He's putting it in the frame of the mirror.

—What?

—The card?

—Where?

—On the left, over the chest of drawers. [*Pause*] He's

opening a drawer. He's taking out a shirt . . . No, a
vest . . . no, a shirt. He's putting it on the table. [*Pause*]
He's looking at it.
—What?
—The shirt. He's unfolding it. He's putting it over the back
of the chair.
Pause
—Is he going to get dressed?
—He's looking out of the window. He's bowed his head.
He's leaning his left cheek on his hand.
—He's got tooth-ache.
—He's coming back to the table. He's putting on his
glasses again. He's looking over at the mirror. He's
taking off his dressing-gown. He's naked. He's looking
at himself. He's feeling—
—What?
—Nothing.
Pause
—What's he doing?
—Nothing. It looks as if he's got a pain in his back. He's
rubbing it.
—What does he look like?
—Thin. Hairy. He's put his left foot up on the chair.
[*Pause*] He's cleaning one of his toenails.
—You're sure there's no-one opposite?
—I can't see, he's in the way.
—Hasn't he drawn the curtain?
—No.
—What's he doing?
—Cleaning his toenails. He's got a varicose vein.
—Is he facing you?

—Almost.

Pause

—What's the book?

—It's yellow. [*Pause*] Now the right foot.

Pause

—What is there before you come to the chest of drawers?

—I can't see.

—You can't see any sign of a book-case?

—No. [*Pause*] Perhaps it's over on the right, before you come to the bed. Or between the bed and the wall. No, I can't see it. [*Pause*] He's found a spot on his calf. He's squeezing it. [*Pause*] He's sitting down again. He's opening the book. He's put his elbows on the table. He's reading. [*Pause*] He's rubbing his back. [*Pause*] Something's happening opposite. Someone's drawn the curtain. [*Pause*] Nothing there. [*Pause*] He's got up. He's taking off his glasses. Going over to the mirror. He's reaching out for the card. He's looking at it. [*Pause*] He's going to put it back in the book. He's going over to the wash-basin.

—Where is the wash-basin?

—To the left of the window.

Pause

—What's he doing?

—I think he's having a pee. Yes. He's running the tap. His bottom's all white. He's looking out of the window. He's going right up to the window. He . . .

—What?

—I think he . . .

—What, what?

—He's still thinking. He's resting his left cheek on his

hand. [*Pause*] He's going over to the bed. He's coming
back to the table. He's putting on his dressing-gown
again. [*Pause*] He's taking the card out of the book.
He's going to put it back in the frame of the mirror.
He's looking at himself in the mirror. He's rubbing his
head. [*Pause*] He's going over to the wash-basin. He's
picked up a bottle. He's pouring something on his head.
—Shampoo?
—Lotion, I should think.
   Pause
—What's he doing?
—Walking to and fro massaging his scalp.
   Pause
—Can't you see what the book is?
—It's yellow. That's all I can see.
—What about the postcard?
—Blue. A view, I think.
—Where is he?
—Over by the bed. [*Pause*] Past the bed. I can't see him any
   more. [*Pause*] Something happening opposite. A hand
   coming out through the curtains. An arm. It's opening
   the window. Taking the pants off the line. And the
   shirt. It's shutting the window again.
—Who is it?
—An arm.
—What's on the right of the window?
—The front of the house.
—No, in the room I mean.
—A chair with a case open on it.
—What sort of case?
—Brown leather.

—Large?

—Medium.

—Can you see what's in it?

Pause

—Papers, I think . . . Yes, a sort of file. And the sleeve of a black pullover.

—Any label on the case?

—Yes.

—What?

—Too small. Hotel label.

—Only the one case?

—There's something sticking out on the right. On the floor. It's too far over. Perhaps it's a bag. Or a box. [*Pause*] He's coming back. I think he must be making the bed.

Pause

—What can there be behind the bed? Can't you see in the mirror?

—No. [*Pause*] He's just thrown his dressing-gown on to the table. [*Pause*] He's going over to the wash-basin with a saucepan. [*Pause*] He's filling it with water. [*Pause*] He's gone back behind the bed again.

—A stove. [*Pause*] What's he taken his dressing-gown off for? [*Pause*] Is he going to wash?

—He's come back and sat down again with the book. He's opening it. He's looking at the postcard. He's getting up. He's picking up the book. He's going to put it on the chest of drawers. [*Pause*] He's leaning his left cheek on his hand. [*Pause*] He's opening the bottom drawer. He's taking out some socks. He's looking at them. They must have a hole in them. He's putting them

44

back in the drawer. He's taking out some others. He's looking at them. They've got holes too. He's taking out some others. Black and white stripes. He's looking at them. He's holding them up beside his face and looking at himself in the mirror. He's putting them back in the drawer. [*Pause*] He's getting some more out. Black ones. He's holding *them* up to his face.

—Is he smelling them?

—No, just looking.

—What's on the chest of drawers?

—The book. A gilt clock. A candlestick. A little animal.

—A live one?

—A sort of little dog made of . . . rubber, I think. [*Pause*] He's going back behind the bed again.

—Still nothing happening opposite?

—No. [*Pause*] He's come back with a cup. Steam coming out of it. He's sitting down. He's trying to drink. It's too hot. He's put the cup down. He's looking over at the postcard. He's put his elbows on the table. He's put his head in his hands.

Longer pause

—Well?

—I don't know . . . [*Pause*] I think he's crying. His shoulders are shaking. Sobs. Yes, he's crying. [*Longer pause*] He's looking for something in his dressing-gown. He's blowing his nose. [*Pause*] He's picked up the cup again. He's drinking, slowly. His eyes are all red. [*Pause*] Something's moving opposite. Someone just opened the window.

—The same arm?

—I didn't see. [*Pause*] He's still sipping. He's looking at

the postcard. [*Pause*] He's put the cup down. He's got up. He's looking at the shirt on the back of the chair. He's picking it up. It must have got crumpled, he was leaning against it. He's thrown it on the floor. [*Pause*] He's bending down to pick it up. He's putting it in the case. He's going over to the chest of drawers. He's opening the top drawer. He's getting out a blue shirt. He's putting it over the back of the chair. He's going over to the case. He's leaning his right cheek on his hand. [*Pause*] He's looking out of the window. [*Pause*] He's scratching his stomach. He's taking the shirt out of the case. He's going over to put in on the chest of drawers. He's looking at the postcard. He's going back over to the case. [*Pause*] He's getting the papers out. Yes, it's a file. A big one. [*Pause*] He's going to put it . . . on the table. He's looking over at the bed. He's going over to it . . . I can't see him any more. [*Longer pause*]
He's just thrown a towel at the mirror. The little dog's fallen down. [*Pause*] He's running across. He's getting hold of the postcard. He's looking at it. He's kissing it.
Pause
—When did it come?
—Yesterday, or the day before yesterday, or before that.
—But wasn't he here?
—It would have been waiting for him when he got back. [*Pause*] He's putting it back in the book. [*Pause*] He's leaning his left cheek on his hand. [*Pause*] He's going over to the wash-basin. He's wetting his face. He's picking up a tube. He's putting something on his face. He's going to shave.
—Why did he go away? [*Pause*] Did he have that case

before? [*Pause*] Can't you see what it says on the label?
—No.
—Why didn't he tell his niece?
—She doesn't know. She thinks he went away on business.
—What sort of business?
—To see his lawyer perhaps. [*Pause*] He's going back behind the bed. [*Pause*] He's coming back with the saucepan. He's emptying it into the basin. It's still steaming. He's looking for something. [*Pause*] He's going over to the case. He's poking about in it. He's going back to the basin. He's taking his razor out of the toilet case.
—Is he going away again?
—According to the niece, yes.
—Hasn't she any idea where he goes?
—She says not.
—How does she know he's going away again?
—That's how it was the last time. And the time before that.
—When?
—He doesn't do anything else now but come and go.
—Does she know anything about the card?
—I didn't ask her.
—What about the file?
—Still on the table.
—What is it?
—Papers.
—What about?
—He's going over to the case again. He's poking about in it. [*Pause*] He's gone back to the wash-basin.
—Papers about what? [*Pause*] And the niece?
—What about the niece? He's going over to the chest

of drawers. He's picking up the little dog. He's putting it back on the chest of drawers. He's going back to the wash-basin.

—Has he finished shaving?

—Not yet. [*Pause*] He's got hairy shoulders. [*Pause*] It's a bag, beside the case. [*Pause*] There's a big crack in the wall under the window.

—Has the niece been here since he moved?

—It was she put the curtains up. Grey with pink roses. [*Pause*] He's finished now, he's rinsing his face. [*Pause*] He's emptying the basin. He's cleaning it out with his hand. He's picked up a bottle. He's rubbing something on his face. [*Pause*] He's brushing his hair. [*Longer pause*] He's going back to the table. He's looking at the file. He's sitting down. He's opening the file. He's putting on his glasses. He's put his elbows on the table. He's reading.

—Why did he move?

—I don't know. [*Pause*] Something happening opposite. The arm's coming out from behind the curtain. It's opening the window. It's putting a handkerchief on the line. [*Pause*] It's just shut the window. It's a man. He's got a moustache. He's looking out of the window.

—Is he looking over here?

—No, down into the street. He's leaning on the sill. He's wearing a white shirt and a bow tie. About in his forties. Maybe fifty. Maybe thirty.

—And he's not looking over here?

—He's interested in something in the street.

—Is the niece still at the villa? He hasn't sold it?

—No. She's still there, says she's cleaning up.

—And the nephew?

—He hasn't been there for a long time.

—I'd heard he'd been back recently.

—Idle gossip.

—They ought to watch out for the old boy. [*Pause*] What's he doing?

Pause

—Reading the file. [*Pause*] He's writing something.

—In the file?

—By the side. A little book.

—Is he still naked?

—Yes. [*Pause*] He's getting up. He's taking off his glasses.

—Why was the file in the case? Do you think the lawyer knows?

—He's going back behind the bed. [*Pause*] The screen's moving. He's pushing the screen forward. He's hiding the case. [*Pause*] [*Hastily*] He's coming over to the door. Get back.

Longer pause

—Why worry, he couldn't have heard us.

—He might have come out. [*Longer pause*] He's back in front of the window.

—What's he doing?

—Leaning his right cheek on his hand.

—Can't he do anything else? [*Pause*] Anything happening opposite?

—The chap's not there any more. He's drawn the curtain.

—Are you sure he wasn't watching him?

—He was looking down at the street. [*Pause*] Besides, he can't see in here, the sun would be in his eyes. [*Pause*] He's pushing the screen back towards the wall. [*Pause*]

He's picking the bag up off the floor. He's putting it on the table. He's taking a map out of it. A bottle. A little parcel. Some pincers. [*Pause*] He's thrown the bag at the chest of drawers. [*Pause*] He's opening up the little parcel. A sandwich. An orange. He's thrown them at the chest of drawers.

—Is there a waste bin?

—I can't see. [*Pause*] He's folding up the paper. He's putting it in the file.

—The sandwich paper?

—He's opening up the book. He's taking out the postcard. He's getting up. He's going over to the window. He's bending down. He's slipping the card into the crack. [*Pause*] He's scratching at the floor. I can't see very well. [*Longer pause*] He's taken up one of the floor-boards. He's going over to the chest of drawers. He's taking the crumpled shirt. He's rolling it up into a sausage. [*Pause*] He's going over to the window. He's bending down. He's putting the shirt into the hole in the floor. He's standing up. He's looking out of the window. [*Pause*] He's going back to the chest of drawers. He's picking up the little dog. He's going over to the window. He's putting it in the hole.

—Is he mad?

—He's putting the floor-board back. He's leaning his left cheek on his hand. [*Pause*] He's going over to the table. [*Pause*] He's putting on his dressing-gown. [*Pause*] He's going over to the case. He's taking out the black pullover. He's shaking it. He's going over to the table. He's spreading the pullover out. He's folding it up. He's opening one of the drawers in the chest of drawers. He's putting the pullover away. [*Pause*] He's going back to the window. He's bending down. He's taking the card out of the crack. He's putting it in the case. He's shutting the case. [*Pause*] He's putting it behind the screen. [*Pause*] He's going over to the chest of drawers again. He's opening the drawer. He's taking the pullover out again. He's taking a pair of scissors out of the drawer. [*Pause*] He's cutting one of the sleeves off the pullover. Now the other one. [*Longer pause*] He's cutting the pullover in half. [*Longer pause*] He's picking up the pieces. Carefully. He's rolling them up into a sausage.

—He's going to put them under the floor-board.

—He's going over to the window. He's opening it. He's thrown the sausage out. He's shutting the window as fast as he can. He's run behind the bed. [*Longer pause*]

—No point in all this. Why stay?

—Orders.

—Whose?

—He's going over to the screen. He's getting the case out. He's opening it. He's taking out the postcard. [*Pause*] He's looking at it. He's going over to the table. He's putting on his glasses. [*Pause*] He's re-reading the card. He's turning it over. He's peering at it. [*Pause*] He's putting it down on the table. [*Pause*] He's putting his head in his hands. [*Pause*] He's sitting down. [*Pause*] He's taking off his glasses.

Longer pause

—Well?

—He's crying again. He's shaking all over. [*Longer pause*] He's picked up the card. [*Pause*] He's tearing it up. Once across. Twice. Three times. [*Pause*] He's looking at the pieces. He's crying. [*Longer pause*] He's looking for his handkerchief. He's found it under the table. He's blowing his nose. [*Pause*] He's picking up the pieces. He's arranging them on the table. [*Pause*] He's getting up. He's going over to the chest of drawers. He's opening the top drawer. He's taking a tube out. And a sheet of paper. [*Pause*] He's sitting down again. [*Pause*] He's sticking the pieces together on the paper.

—Who gave these orders?

—Something is happening opposite. The man's opening the window. He's wearing dark glasses. He's looking down into the street.

—Answer, who gave these orders?

—It was before . . . when it all began . . . Ought to have . . . [*Pause*] He's looking for one of the pieces. He's picking it up off the floor. He's sticking it on. [*Pause*] The other one's looking over here. [*Pause*] He's turning round. Someone's passed him a pair of pants. He's hanging them on the line. [*Pause*] They're handing him some socks.

—Who?

—I can't see. He's hanging out the socks. [*Longer pause*] He's finished sticking the card together. He's looking at it. [*Pause*] Ought to have . . . helped him . . . he didn't want help . . . been with him . . . impossible . . . changed something . . .

—What's that you're saying?

—He's putting the sheet of paper into the file. [*Pause*] He's looking through the file. [*Pause*] He's reading. He's noting something down in the little book.

—Hasn't he ever had anyone? [*Pause*] Answer, hasn't he ever had anyone?

—Well . . .

—What?

—I don't know.

—He used not to be alone?

—He's getting up. He's taking his dressing-gown off. He's going behind the bed. [*Pause*] He's coming back. He's put his socks on. He's going over to the case. He's putting it back on the chair. He's going over to the wash-basin. He's picking up the flannel. The soap. He's washing his arms. His chest. He's got hold of the towel. He's drying himself.

—Doesn't he wash anywhere else?

—He's going over to the window. He's looking at the curtains. He's touching them. He's seeing if they work.
Pause

—Are they drawn?

—No. He's looking out of the window. [*Pause*] He's jumped back.

—Something happening opposite?

—I couldn't see, he was in the way. He's over by the case. Nobody opposite. The wind's started to blow. The pants are flapping. There's only one sock there now.

—Where?

—At the window opposite. [*Pause*] He's putting the case back on the floor. He's sitting down on the chair. He's put his head in his hands.

—I'm getting fed up with this.

—You can go.

—Are you staying?

—He's getting up. He's bending down. He's taking up the floor-board in front of the window. He's taking out the little dog. He's going over to the chest of drawers. He's putting it down on it. [*Pause*] He's looking at himself in the glass. He's going back to the window. He's bending down. He's taking the shirt out of the hole. He's putting the floor-board back. [*Pause*] He's going back to the chest of drawers. He's opening the top drawer. He's putting the shirt back in the drawer. [*Pause*] He's reaching out for the file. [*Pause*] He's hesitating. [*Pause*] He's picking up the file. He's going over to the case. He's putting the file back in it. He's shutting it. [*Pause*] He's going over to the table. [*Pause*] He's going back to the case. He's opening it. He's looking through the file. He's taking out a paper. It's the sandwich paper. He's shutting the case again. He's going over to the chest of drawers. [*Pause*] He's bending down. He's picking up the bag. The sandwich. The orange. He's putting them on the table. He's doing them up in a parcel again. [*Longer pause*] He's putting it in the bag. He's putting the bottle back too. The map. The pincers. [*Pause*] He's picking up the bag. He's going to put it under the chair he put the case on. He's coming back towards the table. He's sitting down. He's looking over at the mirror. [*Longer pause*] He's looking for something on the floor. [*Pause*] Under the table.
Pause

—It must be the pullover.

—He's getting up. He's going over to the window. He's bending down. He's lifting up the floor-board. He's searching in the hole. [*Pause*] He's putting the floor-board back. He's standing up. He's reaching out for the handle of the window. He can't bring himself to open it. [*Pause*] He's jumped back.

—Something happening opposite?

—He's bending down. He's turning towards the table. He's crawling to it on all fours. [*Pause*] He's hanging on to the chair. [*Pause*] He . . . he . . .

—Can't he get up?

—He's got up. He's passing his hands over his eyes. [*Pause*] He's going over to the wash-basin. He's picked up a glass. He's filling it with water. [*Pause*] He's emptying it into the basin. [*Pause*] He's taking something off the shelf. In the palm of his hand. [*Pause*] He's putting his hand to his mouth. He's thrown back his head and swallowed. [*Pause*] He's coming back to the table. He's putting on his dressing-gown. He's turning towards the mirror. He's smoothing down his collar. He's tying his belt carefully. [*Pause*] He . . .

—Is he expecting someone?

—He looks very strange . . . As if he were swaying. [*Pause*] He's folding the blue shirt on the table. [*Pause*] He's sat down again. He's putting his elbows on the table. He's staring into space. [*Pause*] He's leaning on the file. He's looking up at the ceiling. [*Pause*] I think his eyes are shut. [*Pause*] His head's fallen to one side.

—He must be going to sleep.

—His arms have dropped down at his sides. [*Pause*] His mouth . . . He's as pale as . . . [*Pause. Excitedly*] The tablet!

—He's poisoned himself!
—*Shouting, normal voice*] Open the door! Open the door! Open the door!

    [*Repeated hammerings at the door*]

Interview I

—With the intention of writing about it?

—Intention, it wasn't really an intention, more the feeling that . . . the feeling, a feeling. . .

—A feeling that you might try to talk about it?

—You could say that.

—When did you begin?

—A good ten years ago . . . or perhaps I'd begun even before, say about ten years.

—So it was a long time after the event, only memories?

—Yes.

—Did you have difficulty in assembling them?

—Not in assembling them, in what shall I say . . . arranging them, sorting them out.

—You knew him well, Mortin?

—Yes . . . [*Pause*] I knew everything he did and when he did it and how, by heart.

—You mean it was possible for you to imagine everything he did without seeing him?

—Yes . . . I didn't see him all the time, he didn't like being disturbed . . . but in the beginning before I got on his nerves he used to let me . . . I stayed there all day, I had time.

—When did you start to get on his nerves?

—Not long after we met, six months perhaps, yes six months.

—And it was then you started to imagine his days?

—Yes.

—But you went on seeing him from time to time?

—Once a week, then once a fortnight, then once a month
. . . until I got on his nerves too much, then I didn't go
back any more.

—Did you go on imagining his days for long?

—Yes, a long time.

—How long?

—I don't know . . ten years perhaps.

—Until you decided to get it all out of your system by
writing your recollections down?

—I told you it wasn't a decision it was . . . [*Pause*] Besides
I'd already started, odd sentences I'd put away in a
drawer . . . not that that got me anywhere, I can't write.

—Why do you say you had difficulty in sorting out what
you remembered?

—Because I did.

—Explain.

—I didn't know whether I ought to remember the days
themselves or what he'd said or done on some particular
day . . . If I ought to begin with the first day and tell all
about that and then go on to the second and so on like
that to the end . . . or if I ought to start by saying something about him, his health for example and then go on
to the things he used to say and then say something
about when I first started to get on his nerves and then
go on to the visits getting fewer and fewer . . . [*Pause*]
Because then I didn't see him as I used to see him, I
mean he was different . . . Ought I to be asking myself
whether this new Mortin was the same as the old only
I hadn't seen him when I used to see him or actually a

different one and if so how many of them were there . . .
Yes, it was impossible, everything got mixed up . . . I
made twenty, thirty attempts.

—Until finally you threw them all down the well?

—Yes.

—And then you felt free?

—At first yes, then not.

—Did you ever resume your experiments?

—It wasn't any good, I can't write . . . [*Pause*] But to forget
all that . . .

—What did you have to say about his health?

—It was just an example that came into my head.

—Was it good?

—Quite, but he often had headaches . . . One lasted several
days, I had to call the doctor, he said rest and some
medicine we bought.

—Would Mortin stay in bed on such occasions?

—Only the time I said, not otherwise.

—Describe a day in Mortin's life.

—When I arrived I'm talking now about the beginning
he'd just got up it was eight o'clock, he was in his
dressing-gown, a brown dressing-gown with a yellow
collar and the cuffs . . . He said he'd had it twenty years
it must have been true, very dirty but he liked old
things . . . and Moorish slippers you could hardly walk
in . . . [*Pause*] He'd be in the kitchen making coffee,
when I arrived he'd put an extra spoonful in the pot . . .
I'd say I'd had some already but he'd say it won't do
you any harm . . . In the beginning that is, afterwards
he didn't insist . . . [*Pause*] I remember the first time he
didn't add another spoonful just said too bad and the

second time he didn't say anything, he took his cup out on the terrace . . . That day there were some pigeons squabbling, he said these pigeons foul everything, we ought to get rid of them . . . Or was that another time . . . [*Pause*] You see the different times are getting mixed up already.

—Keep to when you first used to go. After he'd had his coffee.

—After he'd had his coffee I used to wash up the cups and he used to go and get dressed, then I read the paper on the terrace or in the study . . . that is on the terrace in the beginning, it was still fine, afterwards in the study but I think by then I was only washing up one cup.

—Don't go into unnecessary detail.

—When he'd finished getting dressed he used to tell me what I could do, for example, clean the kitchen or rake the garden or do some shopping, things like that.

—Where did you go to do the shopping?

—The village.

—Far?

—A mile and a quarter, walking.

—Did Mortin use to go there too?

—Sometimes, but not so much when I was there.

—Did the tradesmen come to the house for orders?

—To deliver them.

—How did he order?

—By telephone.

—What sort of thing did you go to get for him?

—Things he'd suddenly run out of, that he'd forgotten to order . . . He would have done without them, of course, it was only that I insisted.

—You worked for him in a sense?

—I'd have been quite willing, but not him, he saw I liked doing it . . . he didn't pay me, of course I wouldn't have wanted that.

—How did you get to know him?

—One day when I was out for a stroll near his place, he said "good morning," and we walked along together for a bit, we talked about some tulip-beds of his, old bulbs and he didn't know they got old . . . he thought they were getting smaller and smaller for want of manure . . . I told him tulips get old like everything else, you have to change them and he asked me into his garden to see them . . . [*Pause*] They were Darwins pink and black, the black were bigger than the pink, they're tougher but they must have been at least three or four years old.

—Was it a big garden?

—About two hundred square yards at the most with a flowerbed each side of the path crossing it and a flower-bed by the house with a little concrete kerb.

—And the house?

—Small, one storey.

—How many rooms?

—Downstairs the kitchen where you went in, to the right it opened on to a small bedroom and to the left into the study, that's to say the room he worked in it was also the dining- and sitting-room . . . In the corner was the staircase and upstairs his bedroom with the bathroom next to it and a boxroom.

—Give a brief description of the study.

—In the middle there was a table with six chairs and facing the door between the two windows the sideboard, that made the dining-room . . . and to the left under one window a red settee with tassels and three armchairs round a pedestal table, that was the sitting-room . . . and at the back on the right under the fourth window his desk and armchair and in the corner the bookcase, books and a little clock that never stopped, he wound it every morning, I think it came to him from his family.

—Wasn't there anything on the walls of this room?

—Pictures, two on each side of the sitting-room window, one in the left corner of the study, that's to say between the window and the corner.

—Do you remember what the pictures represented?

—The first one in the sitting-room was a fishing-port with boats and little fishermen on the quay . . . the other was a winter landscape, pine trees and chalets in the snow, and the one in the study was a Zouave, he had a hole in his tunic that I tried to fill in from behind with sticky paper . . . He said it won't hold but it did hold.

—Go on with the description of the day.

—Where was I?

—The job he used to give you to do.

—Yes, clean the house or rake the garden.

—What did he do while you were doing that?

—He sat down at his desk and wrote without stopping till half-past eleven.

—What was he writing?

—The life of some gentleman he knew, at least I always supposed it was someone he knew . . . he spoke to me about it now and again, he must have known him . . . unless it was a friend of the family but he knew all about him, he had heaps of letters and books as well.

—Do you know the name of this acquaintance?

—Monsieur Mortier.

—What sort of thing did he used to say to you about Mortier?

—That he was very clever, he'd written books and been everywhere but he was very lonely, he often repeated that, very lonely, I didn't understand because he was famous and had a lot of friends . . . it was as if he was trying to make me believe that Mortier was like him, who never saw anybody.

—Did he really never see anybody?

—He still had a niece who used to come to see him, but not often, otherwise nothing.

—Didn't your being there count?

—That was what hurt me most, at the beginning I used to tell myself I should be company for him, that he wouldn't talk so much about being alone . . . but I had to change my tune, I was nothing, I was in the way . . . I had to give it up.

—Go on with your description of his day. He wrote until half-past eleven. And then.

—I brought him in a apéritif, sometimes a tomato-juice, sometimes a port, I'd already begun the lunch, I finished it and served it at a quarter past twelve.

—And you did that every day?

—At the beginning, yes, six months, afterwards less and less as I said.

—What made you do all these things for him if he didn't pay you?

—That's a question I've often been asked.

—Well?

—Well nothing, I liked doing it . . . I wanted to do that for him, it gave me something to do . . . I thought I could be useful, I had the feeling, I said to myself . . . [*Pause*] But you're always mistaken.

—What do you mean?

—You're always mistaken when you think you can be useful, you think you can do something, you can't do anything.

—Have you made other attempts of this kind?

—Not specially but I know very well people all go on in their own way . . . Whatever you try to do for them it doesn't help them.

—Are you thinking of someone in particular?

—No.

—Could Mortin manage without your services?

—He always managed without anybody . . . but what I can say is that all the extra I did couldn't have done him any harm, well-cooked meals, the house cleaned, the garden.

—Did you sleep there?

—He would never let me, I could have, the little bedroom next to the kitchen wasn't used, never let me . . . I went home every night.

—Have you any idea what could have antagonised him?

—Ah, if I'd known, if I'd been able to discover . . . That was the worst, I asked him a thousand times, a thousand times I asked, at first he said it was nothing, that he preferred to be alone, that it was nothing . . . then he said our personalities were incompatible, that it wasn't anybody's fault, as if we'd had words, our personalities, as if I'd taken the liberty of answering back . . . [*Pause*]

In the end he said I got on his nerves or if he didn't say it . . .

—Go on describing the day.

—We had lunch together, at first he used to talk to me, then not, but I thought that might be better for him and I didn't talk any more either . . . I said to myself he never stops talking in a way, writing all the time, but I've often thought about it since. I ought to have asked questions . . . [*Pause*] I ought to have given him a hand, out of that difficulty . . . perhaps it's my fault, I've often thought about it.

—What did he talk to you about at first?

—His work, all he had to write, Monsieur Mortier, the garden, and his niece.

—Did you ever see her?

—Two or three times.

—What do you know about her?

—Nothing very much . . . I don't think he liked her very much, she must have reminded him of his sister and perhaps she came with some ulterior motive.

—What?

—She must have thought he was rich, it's always that.

—Describe her.

—She must have been about thirty but her face didn't flatter her . . . sallow and bad teeth and the way she dressed you'd have taken her for her mother, she was still in mourning after five or six years . . . [*Pause*] She was a schoolmistress, the first time she came she brought a little cake for tea, she was surprised to see me in the kitchen, she asked me who I was, her uncle hadn't said anything to her about me, how much I earned, if I expected to stay . . . [*Pause*] Perhaps she said something nasty to him about me.

—What makes you think that?

—It's all such a long time ago I don't think anything any more.

—Do you remember what made you think it then?

—It was when I was wondering about it a long time afterwards that I came to that conclusion . . . When you keep turning things over in your head, you suddenly see things you think you didn't see at the time.

—Can you put it into words?

—It's of no more consequence than all the rest, it was all in my head and I've learned not to trust it . . . [*Pause*] How can you expect us to find the truth when we're unhappy, you don't know what you're thinking any more, your mind's contaminated.

—Just simply state the idea you had then, however improbable it seems to you now.

—A long while afterwards I remembered that the day after his niece came to see him I found him counting the silver . . . I asked him what was the matter, he looked embarrassed, he said he ought to think about making an inventory of his things, accidents can so easily happen.

—But you thought he didn't trust you?

—Not at the time, it wouldn't have occurred to me, only after . . . and that's what people call the truth, at the time I haven't the faintest idea what I thought, probably some whim of his, then that perhaps his niece had mentioned his will . . . or rather at first that she might have said something about me and then . . .

—Do you remember anything particular about the life of Mortier?

—He'd written books.
—Any detail, any event in his life.
—He'd been to Africa, he'd been married twice.
—Was he still alive?
—I don't know.
—Were the books that Mortin consulted by Mortier or about him?
—There were two or three by him and others about Africa or the army.
—Was Mortier a soldier?
—I think so . . . or perhaps he had been, but in the photograph he was in civilian clothes.
—What photograph?
—In one of the books.
—Did you ever glance through them?
—I didn't like to.
—Go on with the description of the day. Lunch.
—Lunch yes, the life of Mortier, loneliness, the things that never happen . . . [Pause] When I tried to sort all that out I couldn't, I mixed up the times he spoke to me . . . [Pause] To sort things out in my mind I ought to have insisted on sleeping there, I ought to have taken the little bedroom, he would have hated me but at least I should have tried and perhaps you never know in the end he might have accepted me and those things that never happened, he might not have thought about them any more . . . [Pause] Why don't we realize how stupid it is, everyone insisting on dying on his own when with a bit of an effort we could all die together.
—Would you find that more cheerful?
—Just another of my illusions.
—What did you do after lunch?

—I washed up, then I found something to do in the garden or in the house, the afternoon goes quickly.

—Did he go on writing?

—Until four, then he went for a walk along the road, he went as far as the hedge round the land belonging to the mayor, and he came back at a quarter to five, I got his tea ready.

—Didn't you have it with him?

—No.

—Wouldn't he let you?

—I don't like tea.

—Then did he go back to his writing?

—Until seven, when I brought him an apéritif, usually a port ... At first he used to ask me to have one, then not, and I got dinner ready for eight o'clock.

—Did you have dinner together?

—Yes.

—Did he talk to you during dinner?

—At first, then not.

—What time did you leave?

—After I'd done the washing-up, it was usually nine o'clock, at first he used to say, see you in the morning, then not.

—What did he do after dinner?

—Sit in his chair.

—Not doing anything?

—No.

—Do you know what time he went to bed?

—I don't know, perhaps about ten.

—You never had the curiosity to ask him?

—No, I found out one day from the neighbours, they told me they'd s— ... they said he usually goes to bed at ten, the light's switched off.

—You were going to say something else?

—No . . .

—You hesitate . . . Did the neighbours tell you anything else?

—They told me . . . [*Pause*] It isn't important.

—Tell me what it was just the same.

—They told me they'd seen him going towards the village, according to them he used to go there sometimes.

—Had they any idea where he went?

—They didn't know, they just speculated as people do when they've got nothing better to think about.

—What did they suppose?

—That he drank.

—Who were these neighbours?

—An old couple, they're both dead now.

—Mortin never made friends with them?

—They'd stopped seeing each other a long time ago.

—Might these neighbours' suspicions have been based on what they heard in the village?

—They never went out.

—Did they deal with the same tradespeople?

—Yes.

—Mightn't they have told them?

—It never occurred to me.

—Didn't you live in the village?

—No, in the opposite direction on the main road.

—Weren't you ever tempted to try and find out whether what the neighbours said was true?

—I told you all that's not important.

—Say what you know.

—One day I went to the village about half-past ten . . . that's to say I was going home and just before I opened

my door I thought you ought to go to the village . . . I thought what have you got to lose and I turned round and went to the Swan, the bar in the square . . . I ordered a glass of beer and I heard Blimbraz say Mortin might be coming in . . . I asked Blimbraz if he came often, he said sometimes, but the woman who runs the bar said straight away, oh only very occasionally.
—Who's Blimbraz?
—The roadmender.
—Why did the woman butt in?
—That's what I wondered, I didn't insist but later on I asked Cyrille, the waiter, whether Mortin went there or not . . . he said the same as she did, only occasionally.
—Why did the roadmender seem to hope he'd come?
—I asked him again, he said you never know it'd be a free drink, I asked him if he often bought people drinks, he said sometimes.
—Did you speak to the neighbours again?
—Sometimes.
—Did they tell you any more about Mortin's habits?
—These people who've got nothing better to do than talk about everyone else . . .
—What did they tell you?
—Daft tittle-tattle.
—Explain.
—Anything, whatever came into their heads, people can't bear to see anyone living alone, they start gossiping straight away.
—What did they say?
—That I ought to watch out, he must be a neurotic, you can never be too careful with that sort of person, and

wasn't he supposed to have done his wife in years ago . . .
that sort of thing.

—Was he married then?

—He'd been a widower for a long time when I knew him.

—How long?

—About ten years.

—How did his wife die?

—She drowned herself in the river.

—Did the neighbours know her?

—Yes.

—What did they say about her?

—That she was unhappy because of him, you could see
it more and more, she used to be cheerful before and
neighbourly and then gradually she changed and didn't
want to see anybody any more.

—Why did the neighbours think it was Mortin's fault?

—Why, why, people don't ask themselves why, they just
say anything and when a woman changes it's always the
husband's fault.

—Did Mortin talk to you about his wife?

—Never.

—Did you hear anything else about it in the village?

—Nothing much.

—The same suspicions about Mortin?

—It depended, some said he ought never to have got
married, others that he wasn't responsible for his wife's
death . . . most of them didn't bother about it any more,
after ten years people find something else to talk about.

—Didn't you go back to the café to try to find out whether
or not he did drink?

—I went back but I only saw him once a long time after
I'd left.

—Was he or was he not intoxicated?

—No, he bought me a drink, we talked a bit and he went.

—What did you talk about?

—About his work and his niece.

—Did you see her again?

—Once, two or three years after I left, I came just on the offchance, I disturbed them . . . I stayed out in the kitchen, I peeled some potatoes . . . she came out and told me to leave it, she'd see to it herself and I went.

—Did you go back again after that?

—Yes.

—For long?

—A year or two, I don't remember.

—What did you do there the last times you went?

—I peeled some potatoes or did a bit of cleaning . . . [*Pause*] I didn't like to get a meal for him any more, one day he'd said my cooking made him ill.

—When you first began to write down what you remembered, what form did you adopt?

—I don't understand the question.

—Did you finally arrange your recollections chronologically?

—What do you mean?

—You said you didn't know whether you ought to talk about the days one after the other or about your conversations or about his habits.

—That's right, I didn't know.

—What arrangement did you finally adopt?

—I told you I didn't know, I tried, I couldn't get anywhere . . . in the end I chucked it all away.

—You mean what you threw away was set out in several different ways?

—If you like.

—Was it because you couldn't make up your mind about how to set it out that you threw what you'd written away?

—Yes.

—Do you remember any particular difficulty, any one thing that gave you special trouble?

—I told you it was the days or the ideas . . . One day I'd realize that I'd said a certain thing already, or rather I'd wonder whether I hadn't put it in already and I'd read it all again and find I had it in already in a different way . . . I couldn't tell which was the right one, I'd correct one and the next day I'd correct the other and often what was left was not so near the truth as what I'd put in the first place and didn't go with all the rest . . . Then I'd copy out the first again without the corrections and I didn't dare tear up the others in case they came to seem better later on . . . [*Pause*] I kept it all, in the end I got completely confused, it was as if I was talking about three or four different people. . . I'd think dreams are often significant as well and try to remember them, there were some very old ones I wrote down and all of a sudden as I was writing them I'd think they weren't dreams, it happened . . . Sometimes I couldn't remember which it was any more, I'd have to stop, and when I came back to it afterwards I realized it was just something I'd imagined but truer than what happens . . . but when I read it over again I'd wonder whether I hadn't invented the whole thing, I couldn't sleep any more . . . [*Pause*] I'd go back and hang about outside the house and I could see that it really existed, I recognized the kitchen, I even saw him writing through the window . . . [*Pause*]

Once I nearly cried out because I suddenly felt as if I was with him, I was talking to him and I was just going back into the kitchen to do something I'd forgotten . . . When I realized I was just out there in the road imagining it all I came over dizzy and fell down.

—Wasn't there one aspect of the situation that you found more difficult to write about than the rest?

—The first few days after I realized he didn't want me to stay.

—Was there some particular thing?

—I told you I could never discover.

—Among all the possibilities you thought of was there one that seemed more probable than the others?

—For a long time I thought it was the day I burned the omelette . . . I had to make another one without any mushrooms, perhaps he'd been looking forward to the mushrooms, his niece brought them, they were from the family garden . . . he didn't say anything, but I thought afterwards he must have been annoyed, he never lost his temper, but that only made it more difficult, I never knew where I was . . . [*Pause*] Then I thought he couldn't have minded about that because he didn't like his niece much but I'd seen him a few days afterwards with the dictionary open at the page about mushrooms . . . and another day he brought some in with him when he came in from his walk, he asked me if they were the same, they were poisonous . . . [*Pause*] Of course I didn't think of it at the time but afterwards looking back . . .

—Anything else apart from that?

—I'd told him one day he ought to have the path paved, he didn't think it was necessary, I said I got my feet muddy and he said it wouldn't be for long . . . Did he mean the bad weather or had he made up his mind to send me away . . . [*Pause*] Perhaps he had made up his mind because not long after that he told me one morning not to make so much noise when I came in, I asked him when I'd made any noise, he said every morning and then something else I didn't quite catch . . . I thought afterwards it might have been it won't be for long again but at first I thought he only said it won't be for long as if to say I hope it won't be for long, I hope you'll be more careful in future . . . It was only afterwards I realized they both meant he'd made up his mind.

—Anything else?

—He was getting into the habit of muttering to himself at meals . . . I asked him at first what was the matter, he answered nothing at all, my work's giving me trouble . . . Or he'd get up and go and fetch a spoon or the salt instead of asking me and I was stupid enough to think it was just absentmindedness . . . until one day he said he'd rather I only came once a week and so on till the end . . . [*Pause*] But you don't know what it's like not to know . . . it wasn't that I didn't ask him, I didn't do anything else and he'd say it wasn't anything, it wasn't anything . . . [*Pause*] For all that there wasn't any question of my coming every day any more . . . It was then that I began one day to go over in my mind about the mushrooms and I took my courage in both hands and asked him if it was that that had turned him against me . . . he laughed right in my face and said what do you take me for, a lunatic . . . I didn't ask any more.

—Did you put that all down in your manuscript?

—Yes.

—Your various doubts and his answers?

—Yes, I told you that was what was the most difficult . . . I didn't know whether I ought to put what I'd thought at first or what I thought then . . . if I ought to put I wonder whether I'm mistaken, or whether I ought not to write that, just think it . . . and it got so difficult I thought I was going crazy . . . I said to myself, leave it now, I tried but always went back to it . . . [*Pause*] Until the day I decided to throw it all away.

—Why did you throw it down the well instead of burning it?

—I don't know . . . just an idea . . . I tied it all round a stone and went and threw it in.

—And you were saying that soon after you regretted what you'd done?

—I didn't say that.

—Didn't you say you felt free at first, then not?

—Yes, but I couldn't have fished the papers out again.

—So you did regret having thrown them away?

—No, I didn't regret it.

—You felt relieved?

—It wasn't as simple as that . . .

—What do you mean?

—Having failed the first time didn't mean I couldn't try again . . . ought I to have tried again . . . all those things, they were still there . . . perhaps I could have . . .

—And *did* you ever try again?

—I told you, no.

—Just because you couldn't write?

—Yes and then he died, there was no point any more . . . [*Pause*] Suddenly I saw there was no point any more . . . all that time I'd been on the wrong track . . . the truth was that he was dead . . . what could I . . .

Interview II

—It must be . . . it must be . . . twenty years ago . . . yes twenty years.

—Would it be indiscreet to ask how old you were then, madame?

—I was forty . . . that's to say forty-two or perhaps nearly forty-three . . . yes it was spring and my birthday . . .

—How did you know that Monsieur Mortin was looking for staff?

—From the paper . . . yes it was the paper . . . I came across it one morning by chance and I said to myself Noémie you must go and see this gentleman straight away.

—So you're called Noémie? That's a very romantic name. Is that what Monsieur Mortin called you?

—Yes monsieur.

—What was your situation at the time you saw the advertisement?

—Situation . . . situation . . . I don't quite . . .

—Were you single, had you been in service before?

—I was a widow, monsieur, I'd been a widow for ten years . . . my husband died of a heart attack and I . . .

—What did your husband do?

—We had a little watchmaker's business . . .

—Where you happy?

—Was I happy? . . . happy . . . [*Pause*] Life was all over for me when he went, yes all over.

—But you still had a good long stretch left in front of you, Madame Noémie.

—A long stretch yes . . . but I don't know whether you realize, monsieur, I've had to pay for all the happiness I had with Edouard . . .

—Do you mean you were unhappy at Monsieur Mortin's?

—Not unhappy, he always behaved very correctly, but lonely monsieur, lonely . . . and for a woman, you know . . .

—There was never any intimacy between you and Monsieur Mortin?

—Oh monsieur.

—I mean Monsieur Mortin never took you into his confidence, didn't talk to you?

—He didn't talk much at all, you always felt you were disturbing him.

—And his attitude didn't change in all those eighteen years?

—He was always the same, always very correct, he never got cross about anything . . . [*Pause*] Except perhaps once when I made a mistake on the telephone and told someone he was out . . . yes, he was cross that time, I was very ashamed to have made such a mistake.

—Did you always answer the telephone?

—Yes and some days I was supposed to say he wasn't in and that morning he'd told me to say he was in and I got confused for the moment and said no on the telephone.

—It must have been an important call then?

—Yes it was important but I can't remember very well now . . . [*Pause*] I think it was a gentleman who was leaving, they had some business.

—Tell us about your first interview with Monsieur Mortin.

—It's all such a long time ago . . . [*Pause*] I must have come
by the morning bus, it was a manservant opened the door
to me, he showed me into the kitchen and went to find
Monsieur Mortin.

—Did this manservant stay on when you came to work
there?

—No, it was him I was to replace.

—Did he tell you why he was leaving?

—No, I never saw him again.

—Did Monsieur Mortin say why the other man was
leaving?

—No, he never said anything to me.

—Were you the only servant?

—Yes monsieur.

—So you didn't do only the cooking?

—No monsieur.

—So in fact you were his housekeeper, not merely his
cook?

—Housekeeper, housekeeper . . . no that's not the word
. . . cook-general, more like.

—What impression did he make on you when you first
saw him?

—Impression . . .

—Speak up please. What impression did he make on you?

—You mean . . .

—Did you think he seemed cold, did he smile at you, did
he ask about your previous jobs?

—I think he asked me whether I'd been in service before
and I must have told him that was the first time . . . but I
don't remember what impression . . . [*Pause*] I mean he
was just like he always was.

—Do you remember what his reaction was when you told him you hadn't been in service before?

—He'd have preferred someone who had been but I expect he could see I wasn't just a girl, I'd had experience.

—Monsieur Mortin lived alone, didn't he?

—All alone, yes in that great house . . . [*Pause*] Of course he had a nephew who came to see him now and again and sometimes he might stay the night . . . Monsieur Louis.

—Could you give us a brief description of the house?

—It was a ten-room villa with all modern conveniences as they say but there were a lot of things that didn't work properly any more . . . the heating for example it had needed a new boiler for years, he refused to have one put in, he said it was quite good enough as far as he was concerned but in the winter he caught cold and my rheumatism . . . [*Pause*] In the end we only used four rooms.

—Which ones?

—The sitting-room, the kitchen, his bedroom and my bedroom . . . the other rooms were shut up, the dining-room and the smoking-room downstairs and the four other bedrooms upstairs, except when Monsieur Louis stayed, he used to have the blue room.

—And you never had anyone to help you with the work?

—In the last few years we had a charwoman come in on Mondays, she did the rough work, I couldn't manage it any more on my own.

—Did anyone look after the garden?

—Monsieur Mortin pottered about a bit as you might say and a neighbour came and trimmed the trees and did some weeding now and again . . . but it wasn't looked after properly, at the beginning there was a gardener every Saturday but then . . .

—Would you mind speaking up a bit. Then?

—What was I saying?

—You were saying the gardener used to come every Saturday.

—Yes he used to, but then Monsieur Mortin said it was too expensive.

—How did your employer spend his day?

—I'd go and knock him up at eight o'clock and he came down at half-past and had his breakfast.

—Where did he have it?

—In the sitting-room . . . he did everything in the sitting-room . . . meals and work.

—How was it furnished?

—In the middle there was the side-table from the dining-room, we moved it in there the last few years . . . the side-table was big enough for one person, even for two, I served his meals on that.

—What other furniture was there in the sitting-room?

—On the right on the far side there was his desk, that had always been there, and on the left the big settee and the period armchairs and the bookcase . . . and in front of the fire-place the two big easy-chairs, they needed re-upholstering, the horsehair was coming out all over the place but Monsieur Mortin clung to his memories he said, that was how he wanted his furniture and that was how he was going to have it.

—What did he do after breakfast?

—In the summer he went for a walk round the garden, in

81

F

winter he started work straight away . . . [*Pause*] He did
a lot of work you know . . . books, my goodness all his
books . . .

—Do you know what he used to write, were you interested?

—Yes indeed I was interested, I always wanted to ask him
but he didn't like people to ask . . . [*Pause*] I asked him
one day to lend me one of his books, he said poor
Noémie you won't be able to understand a word, but
I wanted to try just the same and he lent me one and
I read it.

—Which one?

—The one about Monsieur Mortier, the life of Monsieur
Mortier, it was almost the same name as his but not the
same thing . . . he was a soldier in Africa for the colonies
. . . life in the army and the natives and all that, I liked
it ever so much.

—Do you know what he was working on chiefly in the last
years of his life?

—It was still the same, yes had been for a very long time,
the life of Mortier's son I think, but I don't know what
he was . . . perhaps he was a soldier too . . .

—And how did you spend your days?

—All the housework, monsieur, it's not very interesting.

—Who was the charwoman?

—A woman from the village she didn't talk much either.

—Did she have her meals with you?

—Yes but as I said she didn't talk.

—And the neighbour who came in and saw to the garden,
who was he?

—Neighbour . . .

—Did he see your employer, did they talk to one another?

—Not often except when there was something particular
. . . like the fence or about flowers, you see the man
wanted to put some in but Monsieur Mortin said they
wouldn't do anyone any good, I often heard him say
that . . . the man would have liked to, it was extra work
for him, a bit of extra money.
—Was he a gardener by profession?
—No, he'd retired from the railway.
—Were there flowers in the gardener's time?
—The first years I was there, yes, in the bed in front of the
house and the two paths leading to the arbour . . . but in
the end Monsieur Mortin wouldn't have them any more.
—Didn't your employer see anyone else besides this neigh-
bour?
—His nephew as I told you, now and again, otherwise
no, no-one.
—What do you know about his nephew?
—Monsieur Louis was the son of his sister who died, he
was a gentleman . . . in his thirties . . . he was an inspector
I think or something like that . . . he worked in the town
hall.
—When did he use to come and see his uncle?
—Once a month or once every two months it was all
according . . . sometimes he stayed the night, he left
in the morning.
—Do you know what he used to talk to your employer
about?
—I don't know no . . . I didn't know . . . they didn't talk
in front of me.
—Weren't you ever tempted, seeing you felt so lonely, to
try to find out what they were talking about?

83

—I always kept my place monsieur . . . it wouldn't have been right . . . I wouldn't have wanted . . .

—Don't agitate yourself, my dear lady, we don't in the least want to embarrass you, but it's just possible that by chance as you were waiting on them you might have overheard a few words, isn't that so?

—Perhaps . . . at one time or another I may have caught a few words but . . .

—There, you see, and what would you say they were about?

—Lord, I don't know . . . perhaps family matters . . . perhaps they were talking about Monsieur Louis's mother . . . that sort of thing you know . . . but as you say . . .

—Yes?

—To have someone there and hear people talking I certainly liked that.

—There you are, madame, you see. [*Pause*] And do you remember any detail of these conversations, anything that might have struck you?

—No monsieur.

—Try to remember.

—No . . . I don't remember.

—And Monsieur Mortin's nephew, didn't he speak to you either?

—He was rather . . . how shall I say . . . rather proud if you see what I mean.

—Wasn't he grateful to you for looking after his uncle?

—Well . . .

—Was he dissatisfied with something perhaps?

—Well . . . well . . . [*Pause*] One day he said I asked rather high wages considering I didn't have all that much work to do.

84

—Did you tell your employer?

—No monsieur.

—Monsieur Mortin couldn't have agreed with his nephew
since he kept you on?

—No monsieur . . . my wages were very reasonable, some
of the maids round about earned three times as much
again as I did.

—Wasn't there anything in Monsieur Mortin's life that you
remember clearly, something amusing for example?

—I . . . I can't think of anything for the moment . . .
Monsieur Mortin's life was as regular as clockwork . . .

—What time did you serve lunch?

—Half-past twelve.

—You probably did the shopping yourself in the village?

—Yes monsieur.

—And didn't you know anyone in the village, people you
could have had a little chat to?

—One or two I said goodday to . . . the woman in the
grocer's talked yes but it was only her own affairs, I
never spoke about mine . . . I've always been very
reserved, Edouard was always telling me I oughtn't
to be so reserved.

—What did Monsieur Mortin do after lunch?

—He slept for half an hour then he went for another walk
round the garden . . . or else he went to the village . . .
to see his lawyer.

—Did his lawyer ever come to see him?

—No never, Monsieur Mortin liked to go himself, it
made a change.

—What time did he start work again?

—At three o'clock usually . . . or else at five if he'd been to
the village.

—Are you certain he only went to see his lawyer in the village?

—Yes . . . he went to see his lawyer.

—You hesitate. Didn't he have any other acquaintances?

—Perhaps monsieur . . . it was no business of mine.

—Didn't he have any friends at the café, for example? [*Pause*] Do you think he had any friends at the café?

—That wretched café . . .

—He did have other acquaintances you see. [*Pause*] And who was it he saw at the café?

—Ah that wretched café, monsieur.

—Do you mean by any chance that he allowed himself to be led astray there?

—Yes monsieur.

—And did that happen often?

—Often, yes.

—And he probably came home rather tired?

—Yes monsieur.

—And you looked after him?

—I'd rather not talk about that.

—When he didn't go to the café what time did he work till?

—Six o'clock, half-past six.

—Do you know who it was he liked to spend his time with in the café?

—I didn't wish to know.

—What time did you serve dinner?

—Half-past seven in the winter, half-past eight in the summer.

—Now tell us something Madame Noémie, try to remember something that will make Monsieur Mortin come alive for us, some little unexpected detail for example, something out of the ordinary.

—I . . . I can't think of anything for the moment monsieur, I've got out of the habit . . . [*Pause*] Perhaps I might tell you there was something happened to me that upset me very much . . . something . . .

—Well tell us that then.

—One day I lost my notebook.

—Notebook?

—A habit I'd had since I was a girl . . . my poor Edouard was always laughing at me . . . a notebook where I wrote down little things from time to time . . . and a year before Monsieur Mortin died yes about a year before I couldn't find my notebook. . . I looked everwhere . . . I even asked Monsieur Mortin, he laughed at me of course . . . And after that I didn't write anything down . . . I didn't feel like it any more . . . But I missed it a lot at the time . . . I used to read it over in the evenings for company . . . it was my memory as you might say . . . and after that I noticed I couldn't remember anything any more . . .

—What sort of thing did you write down in your notebook?

—Just trifles monsieur, trifles . . . or a recipe out of the paper . . . or the things Monsieur Mortin used to say to himself . . . yes he used to talk to himself as he worked . . . it gave me something to think over in the evening.

—Do you remember any of the things he said?

—I can't remember now, I haven't written anything down since . . . I don't think I heard any more . . . besides they were very diffcult things, Monsieur Mortin was extremely clever, extremely . . .

—You were very fond of him weren't you ?

—Yes monsieur.

—And you would have liked him to show more affection for you?

—Oh well you know . . .

—But you stayed on because you were attached to him?

—You get into the habit, you get into the habit . . . [*Pause*] What would he have done without me after all that time.

—And that notebook of yours that might have told us all so much, you never found out what had become of it?

—No never . . . and I missed my letters as well, they were in my notebook.

—What letters?

—The letters from my son . . . his last letters . . .

—You had a son?

—Yes monsieur . . . I had . . .

—And he . . . he went too?

—Ten years ago . . . a car accident.

—Would you like to tell us something about him?

—Oh yes monsieur.

—He wrote to you, so presumably he didn't live with you. Where did he live?

—In Germany, he was an engineer, he was clever my Bernard, we gave him a very good education, and so good to me you wouldn't believe, he was supposed to settle there but he was only waiting till he could come back, he couldn't get used to it there, he was counting the days you might say, yes counting the days . . . and he used to write to me . . . I had his letters . . .

—And you say they disappeared too?

—They were in the notebook, inside the back cover . . . his letters, monsieur, I can remember those all right . . .

—And it all suddenly disappeared and you didn't try to

find out how? [*Pause*] Did you suspect something, somebody?

—Who could have been interested . . . no really . . . my savings that was another matter but my notebook . . .

—Do you mean to say your savings disappeared as well?

—Yes monsieur, everything I had.

—And you didn't tell your employer about it?

—I told him about the book . . . I didn't like to mention the money . . .

—It seems to me you were very negligent, you ought to have gone to the police, you might have been able to recover your property.

—I thought it over carefully, monsieur, very carefully . . . in the end I decided not to do anything . . . if I had it would have seemed as if I suspected . . . Monsieur Mortin . . . or Monsieur Louis . . .

—Do you mind speaking up.

—I don't know . . . nobody came to the house . . . yes it would have seemed as if I suspected someone so I decided not to do anything.

—And you kept all this trouble to youself without telling anybody?

—You get into the habit monsieur.

Pause

—You know, madame, I'm almost certain that if you tried hard you'd be able to remember one of the things Monsieur Mortin said, don't you think so?

—I'd have to think very hard indeed . . . and I feel rather awkward here I'm sorry . . . I'd have to think . . . always very difficult things that's why I can't remember . . . [*Pause*] But if you'd like me to talk about my son then

I could tell you about the letter he wrote on the twelfth of December when he said he was earning more money and was soon going to . . .

—It's Monsieur Mortin we want to hear about. [*Pause*] What time did he go to bed?

—Ten o'clock.

—What did he do between dinner and ten o'clock?

—He read books.

—Do you remember which books?

—Books about Africa or geography . . . and the dictionary . . . [*Pause*] But the last few years he used to fall asleep and I had to wake him up to go to bed.

—Was his health good?

—Yes, except for the last few years, he caught cold easily, I used to call the doctor.

—What was the doctor's name?

—Docteur Mottard.

—Was he the one who attended your employer when he died?

—Yes monsieur.

—Did Monsieur Mortin leave you anything in his will?

—No monsieur.

—Did his nephew inherit the house?

—Yes.

—And he didn't ask you if you'd like to stay on?

—He wasn't obliged to . . .

—So you were suddenly left without savings, without anything?

—What can you do monsieur . . . that's . . . what shall I say . . . that's . . .

Interview III

—You are the third person to talk to us about Monsieur
Mortin. Up till now we've been trying . . .
—Where are the other two? [*Guffaw*] I can't see anyone
but me and you and you're not really a person more a
sort of question machine. [*Guffaw*]
—I meant this is the third time we've interviewed someone on the subject of Alexandre Mortin. We've already
heard his manservant, or at least someone who was very
devoted to him, and his cook. So you're the third person
to sit at this table and answer questions about the
writer you had the honour of knowing.
—Drunk I had the honour of knowing, you mean . . .
[*Guffaw*]
—It's nice to see you in such a good humour, Monsieur
Passavoine. [*Pause*] But if you're to help us, let's be
serious for a few moments. You knew Monsieur Mortin
and you can give us very valuable information.
—*Hawks and spits*] All right then, come on, let's be serious.
—Thank you. [*Pause*] Up till now . . .
—But supposing you ask something that makes me
laugh, what do I do then?
—Laugh, of course. But I don't think you'll find our
questions will be particularly comic. [*Pause*] Up till now
we've been trying to give our listeners an idea of the
late Monsieur Mortin's daily life. Today we want to try
to deal with his death. [*Pause*] However, since you've

91

mentioned drinking we'd better liquidate that problem before we go on, so as to have everything quite clear. [*Pause*] You say he drank? You've often seen him the worse for drink?

—I've seen him plastered three or four times . . . perhaps five or six . . . But the people round about always referred to him as someone who drank.

—Which people?

—The people at the café.

—Which café?

—The Chestnut.

—Come now, Monsieur Passavoine, first you say the people round about and then you say the people at the café. It's not the same thing.

—Yes it is—it's the people round about that go to the café.

—You mean people that spend their time drinking together, and usually more than is good for them.

—What difference does that make?

—Merely that a man like Alexandre Mortin may have his weaker moments, but that doesn't mean he's to be regarded as toper, someone whose only aim is to drink himself senseless, someone without any intellectual life left, or any morals, or any other object but oblivion.

—If that's how you look at it . . .

—We're not interested in one aspect any more than another, Monsieur Passavoine. We're just trying to build up an accurate picture. We know from the previous interviews and from the work he left behind him that Alexandre Mortin was a man of conscience and a remarkable writer; probably someone who suffered a good deal too. Because of all this we don't feel the term drunkard is very apt.

—All right, all right, we'll skip it. But he did drink, you can't . . .

—We know. But we must try to avoid hasty judgments. [*Pause*] So you were a neighbour of his?

—I wouldn't say neighbour exactly, no, the Biaules were his neighbours and Blaise Masson . . . I lived four houses down along the main road.

—But according to what we've been told, you quite often had to do with him on the subject of his garden?

—I did work in his garden for a little while, yes. It was long before I retired, let me see, what would I have been, perhaps about thirty then, I didn't turn my nose up at earning the odd shilling in those days. He paid me by the day. The time we haggled over the price! He was as near as—

—Was it a big garden?

—Hardly swing a cat round, four flower-beds and a path to the arbour. A bine if I remember rightly.

—Did you know his wife?

—His wife?

—He'd been married, hadn't he?

—Not that I know of . . . [*Pause. Laugh*] Unless you're referring to . . .

—Go on.

—You'll say I'm not being serious.

—Not if you speak according to your conscience.

—Well . . . Well, I meant Mimi. He used to go with her. I was only a youngster at the time but she caused a lot of talk. [*Pause*] And Mortin wasn't the only one, mark you.

—You never heard that he'd been married?

—To Mimi?

—No, his wife, Madame Mortin.

—Not that I know of. [*Pause*] Where did you get that from?

—We're supposed to be interviewing *you*, Monsieur Passavoine. [*Pause*] We know that Alexandre Mortin was married.

—Well if you know . . .

—And that he was a widower for nearly thirty years. [*Pause*] Did you always live near him?

—No, I lived at Le Bouset before, about twelve miles away.

—So you might very well know nothing about Monsieur Mortin's family status?

—I couldn't help knowing about Mimi at any rate. [*Laugh*]

—You might very well not know that Monsieur Mortin had the misfortune to lose his wife in a tragic accident?

—Accident? What accident?

—We're supposed to be interviewing you.

—I don't know anything about his wife. All I know is, Mimi came to a sticky end. And serve her right.

—How did she die?

—Tablets. Twenty years ago. That's all I know.

—Poisoned herself, do you mean?

—I mean what I say.

—Poisoned herself, that's what you mean, isn't it?

—If that's how you like to put it. They wouldn't give her church burial. Serve her right.

—Monsieur Passavoine, please be careful what you say. [*Pause*] And try to stick to the matter in hand. [*Pause*] We want to put some questions to you about Monsieur Mortin's death. Do you know what he died of?

—He was ill for five or six years. Cancer, they said. The sort that dri—Sorry.

—Weren't there other theories?

—What do you mean?

—All this happened a very long time ago, Monsieur Passavoine. [*Pause*] We have made some inquiries of our own, and it seems that at the time of Monsieur Mortin's death there were certain rumours, suggesting that in a moment of despair . . . or by mistake . . . he took a fatal dose of some drug . . . or some other highly noxious substance.

—What do you mean?

—That perhaps he poisoned himself.

—You wouldn't be getting him mixed up with Mimi by any chance?

—Mightn't you?

—What do you mean?

—I'm suggesting that when you look back you connect Mimi with the rumours that were really about Alexandre Mortin . . . you confuse the circumstances of the two deaths?

—Well I'm damned, are you calling me a liar?

—Not at all Monsieur Passavoine, not at all. Don't get excited. We know very well how difficult it is to remember things exactly. We should quite understand if you'd made a mistake.

—But I haven't made a mistake, I tell you. Mimi took tablets and Mortin died of cancer, for God's sake, the sort that dri—

—Strange, though, isn't it, that the rumours about Mortin should be the same as those you remember about Mimi?

—Believe what you like. Only if you take more notice of rumours as you call them than you do of me I don't see why you go to the trouble of interviewing me at all.

—Now don't get worked up, Monsieur Passavoine. [*Pause*] We very much need to hear what you have to say. Precisely in order to prove that the rumous were false. [*Pause*] You're quite sure that what you say about Mimi is true?

—That she and Mortin were together? Yes.

—That she took poison.

—Tablets. Yes.

—Do you know whether Monsieur Mortin was much affected by her death? Did he seem very upset, do you remember, or start to act strangely?

—They hadn't been together for a long time when she died. [*Pause*] As for strange, he was always that.

—What do you mean?

—Tell you one thing one day and the opposite thing the next. One day he'd want pansies in the borders, the day after forget-me-nots. One day he'd call me by my name, quite friendly, and the next he'd just say monsieur.

—You saw him every day then?

—Just a manner of speaking. One week you might see him quite a lot and the next week hardly at all. The people round about used to talk about that too.

—In the café, you mean?

—In the café, round about—I told you, it's the same thing.

—And what do you know about his niece?

—Which one?

—He didn't have more than one, did he?

—Two, mother and daughter.

—He had a great-niece, you mean?

—He called her his niece too.

—I mean the mother, the one who was a teacher. She was married, then?

—No, that was the snag. But she had a little girl.

—And she came to see Monsieur Mortin too?

—Sometimes.

—Did you see her? How old was she, about?

—Six or seven, just a kid.

—Did she come to see her great-uncle while you were still looking after the garden?

—I don't remember having seen her there, no.

—Where then?

—At the villa with her mother. Her mother didn't pass the time of day with people any more then, thought herself too grand.

—What villa?

—Mortin's, the one he bought after.

—After what?

—After he stopped living in the other house, for God's sake.

—Whereabouts was this villa?

—Over Crachon way, just before you get to the little wood.

—So you weren't neighbours any more than?

—No.

—But you went on looking after his garden?

—No, he took on a proper gardener.

—But you still saw him?

—Now and again.

—Where?

—In the café.

—The same one?

—No . . . the . . . the Chestnut.

—That's what you said the other one was called.

—I made a mistake, the other one was the Swan.

—So Monsieur Mortin used to go to both of them?

—First the Chestnut and afterwards the . . or rather first the Swan and afterwards the Chestnut.

—Was the Chestnut near the villa?

—Yes.

—And did he use to talk to you there about his niece?

—About the little girl mostly, he was very fond of her.

—So Monsieur Mortin moved. [*Pause*] Did you know his servant?

—He only had a cook.

—In the small house or in the villa?

—The villa. He didn't have anyone in the small house.

—Are you sure he didn't have anyone to help, a man who was very devoted to him and looked after the house?

—Am I sure! The times my wife asked if he'd like her to do for him. But he wouldn't have anyone. One day I heard the niece, the mother, say the place was a proper p—

—Let's get this clear. The small house, that is the first, was just a tiny place with three or four rooms at the most?

—Yes. They used to build them on two floors in those days. Now for only three rooms they'd put it all on one level.

—What about the villa?

—Oh, that was quite a different matter. At least fifteen rooms—more for all I know. With a lovely garden and flower-beds like in a park.

—And he didn't have a manservant there before the cook?

—No, I'm sure he didn't. The cook's name was Noémie

and she went there the same time as he did. [*Pause*] Noémie—there's another one that was a bit strange, as you call it. Never said a word to anyone. She'd had a bereavement that had made her a bit funny—a daughter that died in Africa or somewhere.

—Her son. We know. [*Pause*] And what about Monsieur Mortin's nephew?

—He hadn't got a nephew, that I know of.

—Don't you remember someone called Pierre?

—Monsieur Pierre, yes, I remember him. But that wasn't his nephew, that was just a friend that used to come to the villa sometimes.

—How do you know it wasn't his nephew?

—How do I know? Because he wasn't, for God's sake. His name was Karas or Kavas, something like that. He was a foreigner—spoke with an accent. He travelled for some firm. My wife ordered some coffee from him. He was only a young chap, but there were no flies on him when it came to business, I give you my word.

—What age was he?

—I don't know, about twenty-five.

—Noémie gave us to understand that this Monsieur Pierre was Alexandre Mortin's nephew.

—Noémie? Is she still alive?

—I told you, we interviewed her before you. The man-servant too.

—I didn't connect it. [*Pause*] Noémie, think of that . . .

—Yes. She told us about the nephew.

—She must have made a mistake. Unless Mortin called him his nephew, but I don't see why he should have.

—As you weren't such a very close friend of Monsieur

Mortin's, you might have made a mistake too. [*Pause*] Don't you think?

—Damned if I know what to think.

—You see how careful one has to be in making allegations, Monsieur Passavoine.

—Making what?

—Statements.

—Please yourself . . . [*Laugh*]
Pause

—You were saying that in your opinion Alexandre Mortin behaved strangely, or at least let's say inconsistently. Can you call to mind any other example of this besides the contradictory order you mentioned?

—Order, disorder . . . [*Laugh*]

—Answer the question.

—I have to think. [*Pause*] Well, it's not as difficult as all that—take the time he tried to drown himself.

—He tried to drown himself?

—Proper scream, that was. He was still living in the little house, as you call it. He chose a part of the river where the water doesn't even come up to your knees. But of course he was as tight as an—Sorry. It was me pulled him out. He got off with a week in bed. Bronchitis.

—He might have fallen in by accident.

—Not according to Masson. He's supposed to have told Masson one day that he didn't want to go on living. That's what the Biaules said too, said it didn't surprise them. They'd spoken to the doctor, and he said Mortin had the new rastenic, whatever that is. [*Laugh*] Affects the head, apparently. [*Laugh*] So you see what I mean when I say he was a bit funny.

—And you say it was you pulled him out?

—I just happened to be passing and there he was in the dri—Sorry. Not moving a muscle. So I dragged him out on to the bank and gave him a couple of slaps, and he opened his eyes.

—Did this accident take place at about the same time as something else, some serious incident in Mortin's life that might have particularly upset him? Mimi's death for example?

—You're on the wrong track there. I told you, Mimi took her tablets at least ten years afterwards.

—Something else then? Some disappointment? [*Pause*] But probably you wouldn't know. You weren't in his confidence. [*Pause*] Do you remember hearing, it would be much later probably, about a correspondence he was supposed to have had with somebody?

—Correspondence?

—Yes. Everyone knows everyone else's business in a little place like that, surely you must have heard that some time before he poisoned himself Mortin . . .

—But I tell you he didn't poison himself. He died of cancer, the sort that . . .

—I'm sorry. [*Pause*] But wasn't there some talk, at one time or another, about a certain letter that was supposed to have brought on an attack of depression, that might have hastened his death?

—Let me think. [*Pause*] Oh, perhaps you mean the postcard?

—That's it.

—Yes, yes, now it's coming back to me, I did hear something. Some acquaintance of his who'd been to stay at the villa. Sinture the postman must have told you about it . . . [*Pause*] It's true about the postcard though. It wasn't signed apparently. A view of Africa or somewhere. Sinture said it wasn't the sort of card people send.

—What did he mean? People are always sending postcards of views.

—No, he meant people don't write to one another like that. There wasn't anything on it but 'Best wishes' or 'Be seeing you.'

—Are you sure it wasn't 'Goodbye'?

—Perhaps. I don't remember. The daft finicking things you want to know—how can anyone be sure whether they're true or not?

—And the person who wrote the card—did they know who it was?

—Good God no, how do you expect me to remember?

—You remembered the postcard.

—That's right, so I did. I used to know Sinture very well. [*Pause*] You know it's the niece you want to ask about it, the mother, unless of course she's dead too. [*Laugh*] She had the old man watched. She expected to inherit. She wanted to know everything about everything. But she came unstuck there.

—She had him watched, you say?

—According to Sinture.

—Who by?

—I don't know. [*Pause*] But . . .

—What?

—You'll say I'm not being serious again.

—Come on, say it.

—Well, the old boy used to walk about in his room without any clothes on.

—Which room?

—At the villa. [*Pause*] Or it may have been the other. He had another room in the village where he used to work apparently. We always used to wonder what kind of work. [*Laugh*]

—But he still lived at the villa?

—Yes.

—Do you know whether his niece, or nieces, lived there with him?

—No, he was all on his own. Even Noémie had gone. I reckon it was that, being all on his own, that got him down, as they say. [*Pause*] He started to travel. Imagine that. At his age. He'd go off anywhere, any time, even at night. Then he'd come back again a week later, or perhaps only a few days.

—Where did he go?

—No-one ever knew. Not far probably.

—Did you ever hear of him taking things to make him sleep, or for his illness?

—He must have taken something for his cancer, stands to reason.

—I meant his neurasthenia.

—*Laugh*] I don't know anything about that.

Pause

—When he died did you talk to Noémie? What did she say?

—What could she say?

—Did she know anything about his last moments?

—She'd already left. I told you. [*Pause*] Quite a long time before.

—How long?

—Five or six years—all the time he was ill.

—Where did he die?

—In bed.

—At the villa?

—Yes.

—Didn't he have anybody to look after him?

—I think his niece used to come now and again.

—Did she inherit the villa?

—No—Monsieur Pierre. The niece didn't wait for any more, she flounced off to America with her daughter, and died there. Not long after, so they say.

—Why do you say she didn't wait for any more?

—Just a manner of speaking. She was furious but there was nothing she could do.

—And weren't there any comments about her going? Didn't anybody suspect . . .

—Not that I know of. She just went off in a huff. [*Pause*] In any case the old boy had had it.

Interview IV

—How long ago was that exactly, madame—do you remember?

—Eighteen years, monsieur, eighteen years.

—I notice the room is almost empty. Just a chest of drawers and a mirror. I suppose it used to be fully furnished. Can you tell us more or less where the various pieces of furniture stood?

—Certainly. [*Pause*] Here along by this wall was the bed. And here there was a big round table and four chairs. On the left of the window a wardrobe and on the right a bookcase. We moved all that stuff out ten years ago, my son needed it, and I haven't let the room again since. Wait though. [*Pause*] Maybe in Monsieur Mortin's time the bed was here . . . and the bookcase here . . . or else . . . I've had so many tenants, monsieur, and they all shifted the furniture about, and I used to move it back or change it around to suit myself. I used to let other rooms as well.

—So you probably let this room to someone else after Monsieur Mortin?

—Yes, several people . . . An English lady, Madame . . . Madame . . . what was her name . . . Madame . . . I've got it on the tip of my tongue, how silly . . . then a young couple or was that before, oh yes it was before, a young couple, the dirt, you wouldn't believe . . . I had to ask them to go. They shifted the furniture about all over the place, worse than anybody. The girl came from very . . . what shall I say . . . humble surroundings, no education, no idea how to manage, she just let everything go.

—And were there other tenants before Monsieur Mortin?

—Yes indeed. Don't ask me their names . . . But there was a young Italian, I remember . . . the filth, I couldn't describe . . .

—You never know who you're going to get when you start letting rooms.

—Ah, Monsieur, if I could have managed without . . . Mind you, nowadays I have much less trouble, thank heaven, I only let one room. A student, girl of course, extremely clean, extremely well-behaved.

—And so this room hasn't been let for about ten years?

—No, it isn't used any more, I've just left it . . . [*Pause*] My goodness, the dust, I'm quite ashamed.

—Please don't give it a thought—a room that no-one ever comes into . . . [*Pause*] So this is where Monsieur Mortin lived. One can just imagine it. The round table, the bookcase, the big wardrobe . . . Was he here very long?

—Two years. But he didn't actually live here, you know. He only came for one or two days a week. Saturday and Sunday usually. To work. He said he couldn't work quietly any more at home, too many memories, too many worries . . . [*Pause*] Eccentric, he was, there's no getting away from it.

—Eccentric?

—Well, to own a great villa like that and then rent this room to work in . . . He could have worked perfectly quietly at home, he lived all on his own . . . [*Pause*] He used to say it took him out of himself to come here.

Used to say! We couldn't have spoken more than about four times altogether. He was a very unforthcoming sort of man.

—And so for those two years he only worked on Saturdays and Sundays?

—I couldn't really tell you. I left him absolutely to himself as he'd asked me to do. He did his own cleaning and took the key with him when he went.

—So you never actually saw him working at the round table here?

—No, never.

Pause

—And it was in this room that he . . . how shall I put it . . . had that bad turn?

—What do you mean?

—When he tried to . . . er . . . poison himself.

—Poison himself? Monsieur Mortin? Here? . . . I would never have allowed such a thing!

—You never heard it suggested that in a moment of depression . . .

—No, monsieur, no-one's ever poisoned himself in my house.

—You wouldn't have been responsible, of course, my dear lady, even if they had. [*Pause*] So he was always in perfectly good health while he was staying here?

—I can't say whether he was in good health or not, he never spoke. But he was always very correct. Perfectly correct.

—Did you keep in touch with him after he left? Did you see him again?

—No. I don't think he saw anybody much after that. Buried himself in his villa.

—And you never knew anything about the circumstances of his death?

—No. I think one of his nieces looked after him at the end. The villa was left to her, but she sold it straight away . . . I don't know the people who've got it now.
Pause.

—Did Monsieur Mortin have visitors while he was here?

—Good gracious, I've no idea. He used the back door, he could have visitors without my knowing anything about it.

—You don't recall having seen his niece here, for example, or his nephew?

—I know he had a friend who was very fond of him, but . . .

—Do you remember his name?

—Monsieur André, I think it was . . . yes, that's right, André. [*Pause*] He *might* have come to see him here. He was a very distinguished-looking young man. I saw him once or twice in the square with Monsieur Mortin.

—Wasn't he really his nephew? [*Pause*] And wasn't the nephew's name really Pierre?

—André's the name I remember . . . [*Pause*] I hope you won't think me indiscreet . . .

—Indiscreet?

—I remember there was a postcard came here signed André.

—That might have been someone else.

—I . . . I don't think so . . . [*Pause*] Monsieur Mortin . . . [*Pause*] But my memory's so bad . . .

—Do you mean Monsieur Mortin spoke to you about Monsieur André?

—I . . . I don't want to be indiscreet.

—Don't be afraid to speak. We can cut. [*Pause*] What do you know about Monsieur André?

—Well, monsieur, there was an awful scene here in this room . . . [*Longer pause*] It was a Saturday evening. I'd already gone to bed. When suddenly I heard a violent argument. At first I thought it was in the street. Then I got up and went to look at the other rooms, I had four tenants then. [*Pause*] The noise was coming from here. The passage is very narrow and I knocked into a chair that was standing against the wall. They must have heard. The argument stopped. I stood out there in the passage, trembling like a leaf. Then I plucked up my courage and knocked at the door and just said the first thing that came into my head, asked was there anything they needed. Then Monsieur Mortin . . . [*Pause*] But no, he made me swear never to talk about it.

—Don't upset yourself. It all happened a long time ago. We shouldn't dream of using it against him.

—Monsieur Mortin called to me to come in. His voice sounded all queer. I went in, and there he was lying on the floor in front of that chest of drawers. He was holding his left shoulder, and his hand was covered in blood. I rushed over to him. He ought to have been carried over to the bed but I couldn't. He asked me to bring some cold water and a towel. [*Pause*] When I think of it . . . [*Pause*] He'd been stabbed, André had stabbed him with a knife and then escaped out of the window. It was still open. I wanted to call the doctor but Mortin absolutely refused, he kept saying it's nothing, it's nothing, don't tell the other tenants, not a word to anyone. I looked after him as well as I could with boiling water and tincture of iodine, think of it, monsieur, iodine I put into the wound. The pain must have been unbearable. It was a deep wound, just there, between the shoulder and there. Oh it was terrible . . . [*Pause*] And would you believe it he got up all by himself and got into bed. The bleeding was getting less. I gave him a sleeping tablet and sat by him all night. I was frightened to death. Suppose he were to die in my house? Before he took the sleeping tablet he made me swear not to tell anyone. [*Pause*] He slept all night. I changed the dressing twice and he didn't wake. There was still a bit of bleeding but nothing serious. He woke up at seven. He was in a good deal of pain but he could move the arm. He made me promise again not to tell anyone, he said everything would be all right, the wound wasn't as deep as I imagined. When I think . . . [*Pause*] How I dared take the responsibility of not calling the doctor . . . [*Pause*] He was so convincing, Monsieur Mortin, so much in charge of the situation . . . [*Pause*] He got over it in a week. I brought his meals up to him here. He must have been made of cast-iron.

—And he actually told you it was André who had wounded him?

—Yes, I insisted on knowing. It was the least he could tell me. [*Pause*] Such a distinguished-looking boy . . .

—Did he tell you why he'd attacked him?

—No, monsieur, it was none of my business. [*Pause*] I thought about it for a long time . . . It was some woman I suppose . . . When two men fight to the death, and you might almost say it was to the death, what other reason could there be? [*Pause*] Well, would you believe it,

Monsieur Mortin forgave him. He didn't see him again but he forgave him. That's what I call magnanimity.

—And did the postcard come afterwards?

—Yes, more than a year after.

—What did it say?

—You don't think I'd read it, monsieur? I only saw the signature.

—But could you say whether it was a long message, or just a few words?

—I don't know.

—You can't remember anything at all?

—No.

—And did you catch anything of the argument they had?

—No, nothing at all. Just noise, loud voices. [*Pause*] Fortunately for them nobody but me heard them at all. The other tenants were all out. [*Pause*] That frightened me too when I thought about it. None of the neighbours made any sign, nobody suspected anything, no-one asked a single question the next day, not a single comment. You could be murdered in your bed and no-one would know anything about it. I'd have liked to confide at least in my friends but I kept my promise. Monsieur Mortin assured me that André had gone away.

—Where did he send the postcard from?

—Germany was it, or Austria? . . . [*Longer pause*] But if I might ask . . . you mentioned something about poisoning . . . Where did you get these rumours from? Did anyone really believe . . .

—Just vague rumours, madame. There were lots of contradictory rumours about the death of Alexandre Mortin. [*Pause*] Do you know anything else about him—about his relationships with people, for example?

—No. Monsieur Mortin was as secret as the grave. He never spoke. As for visitors I don't know any more than what I've already told you. [*Pause*] Unless . . .

—Unless what?

—I could just say something about his relations with some of the neighbours, if that interests you. I remember he couldn't stand Mademoiselle Meyer. She told me he used to put his tongue out at her whenever he saw her. It was very funny to think of Mortin doing a thing like that.

—What had he got against her?

—Some boring story about a lot of old papers, I didn't believe a word of it. Mademoiselle Meyer was a bit . . .

—Papers?

—Yes. She said she saw Monsieur Mortin one evening carrying a big bundle of these papers in the direction of the cemetery. She'd just been to see a friend of hers. When Monsieur Mortin saw her he stumbled and dropped the papers, and when she tried to help him pick them up he turned on her like a wild beast and wouldn't let her come near. [*Pause*] Another thing was that according to Mademoiselle Meyer the manservant Monsieur Mortin had when he used to live in the small house, this manservant had literary pretensions. She said he'd done some questionable things, got hold of some of Monsieur Mortin's manuscripts. She was supposed to have learned all this from some third party, I don't remember who. She said the manservant was over by the cemetery that evening too. She saw him. She was sure she'd come across some secret that neither of them could afford to have known.

—What secret?

—She was a bit dotty, you know. She claimed they used to fabricate Mortin's writings between them, and said that one of them wanted to destroy them and the other didn't. A ridiculous story, all invented, I'm sure. She used to go on about some well not far from the cemetery where she was supposed to have seen Mortin just going to throw his papers down and the other one holding him back by main force. [*Pause*] I don't see that all this is of any interest. [*Pause*]

—So you say Alexandre Mortin didn't write his books alone and unaided?

—I don't say anything at all, monsieur. All I've done is tell you what Mademoiselle Meyer said, and she was mad, and I don't care who hears me say so. That story about a well always struck me as absolutely ridiculous. What's more she died in the asylum. [*Pause*] Actually, it's quite possible that Monsieur Mortin's bed was over there, between the chest of drawers and the washbasin. [*Pause*] Yes, it must have been there . . . [*Pause*] No, it was by the window. [*Pause*] I should tell you that Monsieur Mortin moved the bed after . . . he may have moved it more than once, even . . . [*Pause*] I saw the room again once or twice while he was here and it looked different . . . But I'm getting mixed up with the tenants who came afterwards too. The worry and trouble they've put me to between them . . .

Pause.

—Mortin could only have worked at the round table, couldn't he? Didn't he leave his papers there?

—I couldn't tell you. It always used to upset me to come

in here. [*Pause*] I seem to remember a few suitcases.
Lying about here and there.

—Did he use them to bring his things here from the villa?

—I don't know. He wouldn't have needed suitcases just
for a couple of nights.

—Did he travel?

—I don't know. But why should he have come here to
pack his cases? No, he was a bit strange.

—Did you know his manservant?

—I saw him once or twice in the town. He was . . . drunk,
monsieur, every time I saw him.

—Has Mademoiselle Meyer been dead very long?

—Three or four years . . . [*Pause*] Don't you really think
she invented all that story?

—She may have misconstrued the facts. But there's no
reason to doubt that there were papers and there was a
well. [*Longer pause*] Did you ever hear anything about
Monsieur Mortin's wife?

—Mademoiselle Meyer did tell me one or two things.
They're of no interest.

—What, though?

—He was supposed to have been left a widower. Twice,
in fact. His second wife was a Mademoiselle . . . wait
now . . . Noémie something. [*Pause*] She died of cancer.

—And the first?

—I think she was a widow.

—You must be mixing up the names. Noémie was the
name of his cook. She's still alive.

—I don't know her. And you know how it is with names
. . . [*Pause*] It hardly matters, does it?

—Do you know what his first wife died of?

—Cancer, I think, I just told you.

—You said that was the second.

—I've got a head like a sieve . . . [*Pause*] What was it
Mademoiselle Meyer used to say? [*Pause*] I didn't believe
it at the time because I was sure that Mademoiselle Meyer
was cracked.

—What did she say?

—She said that Madame Mortin . . . wait, just let me sort
it out . . . the second Madame Mortin . . .

—The first.

—The first, yes, the widow. Is that right?

—We didn't know he'd been married twice.

—Well he had according to Mademoiselle Meyer. The
circumstances of the first wife's death . . . She took
drugs or something. They're supposed to have found
lots of empty tubes . . . Yes, it's coming back to me . . .
The police made inquiries about the chemist. [*Pause*]
Good heavens, how long ago it all is. And I didn't believe
a word . . . [*Pause*] If I were you, monsieur, I wouldn't
pay any attention to the memories of an old woman
like me. Especially as they all depend on the gossip of a
madwoman in the first place. Yes, I don't mind saying it
again, Mademoiselle Meyer was mad, the fact that she
died in the asylum proves it.

Interview V

—Do they still call you Monsieur Cyrille?

—Just Cyrille.

—Have you settled in the village for good?

—Yes. After all there was no reason for me to do anything else, I knew everyone, I was used to it, and not having any family . . .

—Were you an orphan?

—No. I meant not having any family left.

—Are you satisfied where you are now?

—Yes. I've had to do some repairs but the house is still standing.

—House? Do you own a house?

—I got it for a song. It had been empty ever since Monsieur Mortin moved out, and the kitchen . . .

—Is it Mortin's house?

—Yes. The small one.

—So you live in his house.

—He put me in touch with his lawyer while he was still alive in case I should be interested. The lawyer was to let me have it at a special price. I had ten years to make up my mind. In the meanwhile it was supposed to be let but the tenants never came. When I saw the house again it was in an awful state, the floor of the kitchen had caved in, but I took it because it was so cheap.

—If Monsieur Mortin did you this favour he must have known you well? Were you friends?

—Yes. I used to see him every day in the café. He knew how I was placed. He used to be interested in any poor devil who didn't mind tapping him. Fleecing him, even. When he died the big house, the villa, was mortgaged up to the hilt. But *I* never asked him for anything.

—I believe he gave you this first refusal on the small house some time before he died?

—Five years.

—Did he think he was failing? Was he afraid something was going to happen to him?

—Not at all. At least not as far as I know. He never spoke to me about dying, although . . . [*Pause*] No, it was just out of kindness, like everything he did. He wore his heart on his sleeve. And so cheerful always.

—Cheerful?

—He always joked about everything. And he stood everyone drinks. So much so I got him not to come at the same time every day. People would have taken advantage.

—Did he go to the Chestnut too?

—The Chestnut? Oh no. He always avoided the place. He couldn't stand the sight of Rognon.

—The owner?

—Yes. They'd had some lawsuit over a field next to the wood. Mortin lost.

—Was Rognon the mayor?

—No. Trutaz was the mayor at that time.

—And you say Mortin came to the Swan every day?

—Yes. Either at four o'clock, or five, or six.

—You were going to say something else about his death. What were you thinking?

—Was I? I don't know.

—You said he never spoke to you about dying, although...

—Although he might have done, we talked about everything quite frankly, he never made any mysteries. No, he wasn't particularly preoccupied by death.

—Did he talk to you specially, single you out?

—Sometimes there weren't any other customers in the café, so then he'd talk to me. [*Pause*] The stories he's told me—no end to them. I've never known anyone with such a gift of the gab.

—He must have had a special feeling for you, then?

—I don't know. He used to speak to everyone. [*Pause*] But yes, perhaps he did . . . like me.

—As he proved by letting you have the house like that. [*Pause*] Did you only see him at the café?

—Sometimes we used to spend Sunday together.

—Where?

—At his house, or sometimes we went out.

—He asked you to his house?

—Yes. Oh, nothing elaborate. We'd just have a snack for lunch.

—Was his servant there?

—Servant?

—Johann.

—Oh, him . . .

—Didn't you like him?

—Nobody did. Mortin helped him a bit out of charity, no other word for it. *He* wanted to worm his way in, rule the roost, make himself indispensable, he never gave Mortin a minute's peace, the scenes he used to make, talk about a shrew, Mortin got fed up, in the end they stopped seeing each other. [*Pause*] And jealous into the bargain. Mad with jealousy.

—Was he jealous of you?

—Of everyone. Mortin liked to have his friends to see him but *he'd* always spoil things. That's why Mortin used to come to the café.

—Do you mean that if it hadn't been for Johann he wouldn't have come?

—Not so often, probably, at least while Johann was still hanging around. Afterwards he'd got into the habit.

—What friends would Mortin have had to see him if he could?

—I don't know. Me. And his nephew. And his niece, of course—he was very fond of her.

—Do you mean the mother or the daughter?

—His niece wasn't married.

—Didn't she have a daughter?

—I've just said she wasn't married.

—A . . . an illegitimate daughter.

—Mademoiselle Odette? You must be joking. She was the most respectable person imaginable.

—And his friends Pierre and André?

—They were nice chaps.

—Did you know them well? Did they often go to see Mortin?

—I met them mostly at the café.

—So there were really two of them—he did have two friends?

—Yes.

—People confuse them.

—They weren't at all alike. Monsieur Pierre was tall and

dark and thickset, and Monsieur André was very thin
and . . . let me see now . . . I think his hair was light
brown. [*Pause*] At any rate they weren't at all alike.
—And Monsieur Louis?
—That was his nephew. A commercial traveller. Fair, he
was, and dynamic, as they call it.
—You're not confusing him with Karas or Kavas, are you?
—Never heard of him.
—So I suppose after Johann was got rid of the niece came
to see her uncle more often?
—I don't know. But she was very fond of him.
—Were you ever at Mortin's while Johann was there?
—Once. He refused to get the lunch. Of course he wasn't
really a servant, but all the same, to make a scene like
that. He went into his room and slammed the door. I
never went back while he was still there.
—His room? Did he sleep at Mortin's then?
—Yes, the little room beside the kitchen.
—*He* says he never slept there. [*Pause*] Why should he
lie about it after all these years? What's the point?
—Perhaps . . . persecution mania.
  Pause
—Did you ever go to the villa?
—Yes. It was a beautiful house. Especially the garden. But
he didn't look after it properly.
—Wasn't there a gardener?
—At first I used to work in the garden on Sundays, but
then . . . I didn't have time.
—So you were the gardener?
—No, I just gave him a hand.
—Didn't he have a gardener afterwards?
—No . . . at least . . .

—What?

—I think a neighbour did a few odd jobs.

—Think? Surely you know? The garden wasn't just abandoned, was it? [*Pause*] Which neighbour?

—I can't remember his name. But Mortin used to do a bit of gardening himself sometimes. So did his friends.

—Monsieur Pierre and Monsieur André, you mean?

—I don't know.

—Why did Mortin move?

—*Why*? What a question . . . [*Pause*] He didn't like it in the small house any more so he decided to make a change. [*Pause*] It surprised me he should spend so much money on it—the villa was far too big for just him and the cook and in the usual way he hardly spent anything on himself.

—Perhaps he could have his friends or his niece to stay more often? [*Pause*] Was that it?

—Perhaps.

—You too perhaps?

—Weekends.

—Often?

—For a time, yes.

—And then not?

—I didn't have so much spare time.

[*Longer pause*]

—In your opinion, was there anything strange about the way Mortin behaved?

—Strange? I don't follow you. [*Pause*] I told you he was completely open and simple and straightforward. [*Pause*] I reckon it's you who started the idea about strangeness. Asking questions of Tom, Dick and Harry.

—That doesn't explain all the contradictions.

—What contradictions?

—Well, for instance that he was quite simple and straight-forward and talked a lot.

—Who says different? [*Pause*] Of course, if you've been talking to Johann or Noémie . . . [*Pause*] He used to call them his cross. If he didn't feel like talking to *them* . . . [*Pause*]

—Did Johann ever come to the Swan?

—Never. He was the one who used to go to the Chestnut. *And* oftener than he ought to have done.

—Did he really never come, not even to see what Mortin was doing or to ask after him?

—No, I tell you. Even the boss didn't like him.

—But he had friends at the Chestnut?

—I wouldn't say friends. Rognon was hand in glove with him.

—What do you mean?

—Johann was up to all the fishy business in the district. Land, mortgages, wills, he had a finger in everything. [*Pause*] He was a nasty piece of work. I think Mortin was afraid of him.

—What makes you say that?

—I don't know . . . I never really found out . . .

—Didn't you say Mortin spoke to you freely, never hid anything from you?

—Yes but he didn't like talking about Johann if he could help it. [*Pause*]

—Might Johann have been threatening him with black-mail, do you suppose?

—Blackmail? What about?

—I don't know . . . [*Pause*] About his wife, for example. There were rumours.

—I know where *they* came from. [*Pause*] If you want the

truth, Mortin was never married. [*Pause*] The woman who lived with him for a while wasn't his wife. He told me. She died a long time before we met. As I understood it she wasn't quite right in the head, and he took her in out of charity too.

—What about the second woman?

—There was only ever one.

—Do you know who she was?

—Her nickname was Mimi. I remember her, or rather the name, when I was a little boy.

—Do you know what she died of?

—Cancer, I believe. [*Pause*] Actually when I say there was only one woman that isn't quite correct. Mortin's mother lived with him for a long while in the little house. I found a portrait of her, Madame Mortin, in the loft—the heirs forgot about it. She was like him. I hung it in my room. She's wearing a little lace cap and . . .

—And did Mortin talk to you about his work?

—Yes, he talked about it all the time.

—So you know all about his book on Mortier and the other one, in manuscript, about the son?

—Yes.

—What did he tell you about Mortier? Was he a relation, a friend? [*Pause*] Do you know?

—I . . .

—What?

—I don't know what I ought to say, I'm not used, it's a very delicate . . .

—If you know something you can do Alexandre Mortin's work a great service. *He* didn't make it very easy for his critics to interpret it. He didn't leave anything that throws any light on it.

—Well . . . one day he told me that Mortier was himself, he

just invented him so as to be able to tell the story of his youth, and it used to make him laugh when people, like Latirail for instance in the *Fantomiard* . . .

—The what?

—The local paper . . . when they claimed to have known Mortier in Africa or somewhere.

—Had Mortin really been to Africa?

—When he was young, yes, he was there in the army, he'd seen the place but he hadn't made a career out of it as he said Mortier did. [*Pause*] So he wrote his book when he came back, quite young, and he spent the rest of his life trying to write the other one about Mortier's son, but he never could, he said he didn't believe in it any more, for years he kept trying, but he was stuck. [*Pause*] I said to him why don't you just tell the truth, that would be the best way to get free, but he always said transposition, transposition, literature transposes, poetry, art, symbol, I don't know what all, what agony, you could almost say he died of it. [*Pause*] Everything he saw he related to something else for the sake of his novel, a sunset over the wood at Le Furet would become dawn over an oasis, the roadmender's big red face he'd give to an Arab chief, something someone said in the café would turn into some other thing said by some other person . . . [*Pause*] I could never understand it but then I'm not clever. [*Pause*] Why anyone can't just put down what they see and hear. [*Pause*] To understand I used to try to imagine the customers different when I was serving them, but it just spoiled everything, I was fond of my job and sometimes people used words and expressions . . . it took away all the pleasure. Mortin used to say I was sentimental.

Pause

—Will you tell us what he used to say about the son—the son he imagined for Mortier?

—He used to say it was the failure of his life.

—He said that?

—He laughed when he said it, but . . . there was something . . . sad about the way he laughed, and especially the way he kept coming back to it, again and again . . . [*Pause*] He used to call it the child he never had.

—Did he really never have a child?

—No.

—Some old affair perhaps? [*Pause*] In Africa? [*Pause*] You don't know?

—No. He'd have told me. There'd have been no reason at all to hide that from me. Besides if he'd had a child he was too kind not to have left him something in his will. And everything went to the nephew.

—You mean the villa that was mortgaged up to the hilt? That wasn't much to leave anybody.

—That's right, I hadn't thought of that. [*Pause*] No, I'm sure he never had a child. That's the sort of thing friends tell one another. Or that they come to know somehow. [*Pause*] No, the son was . . . was his dream . . . just as others dream of a love they've never experienced . . .

—Now *you're* being poetical, Monsieur Cyrille. [*Pause*] Speaking of children, are you sure about Mademoiselle Odette? We've been told she had an illegitimate daughter that Mortin was very attached to.

—It's not true. [*Pause*] Don't forget that as a schoolteacher she might easily have brought one of her pupils with her, once or even often, Mortin was very fond of children.

—Did you ever see one of the niece's pupils with her at Mortin's?

—No. But Mortin talked to me about them. Mademoiselle
Odette used to tell him how she worried about the ones
who came from poor families, she used to ask her uncle
to help them and he never refused. And the little girls
knew him, he'd often be in the square when they came
out of school and he used to give them sweets. [*Pause*]
He did a lot for the orphanage too.
Pause
—And what do you know about Johann's literary tastes?
—Literary tastes . . . [*Pause*] I never saw any evidence that
he had any. But when it came to plaguing Mortin about
his gifts as a writer . . .
—Mortin complained about him to you, then?
—No. But I knew Johann was a real bloodsucker.
—Was he really writing something?
—I couldn't say. Wanted people to think so, more like.
—Do you know about the business with the well?
—Yes, Mortin was very upset, he did tell me that.
—What was it all about, exactly?
—There was this first . . . first what-do-you-call-it . . .
sketch, draft of the life of Mortier's son, that he'd lent
to Johann. Johann threw it down the well out of spite
when Mortin chucked him out.
Pause
—You said you thought Mortin was afraid of Johann.
What could have been the reason for that, do you think?
—I've told you I don't know. I've often wondered . . .
[*Pause*] It must have dated from a long way back.
They'd met in Africa when Mortin was in the army.
Something must have happened then . . . [*Pause*] Did
Mortin feel bound by it? Out of gratitude? [*Pause*]
At any rate Johann exploited it.

—What sort of thing? Can you imagine what it could have been?

—N . . . no.

—Not the least idea?

—No.

—Did the niece have any suspicions?

—If she had it wouldn't have been like her to say anything. She was very discreet.

—We must remember that apparently Johann never did reveal anything, when he wanted to get his own back he resorted to the childish trick of destroying the manuscript. [*Pause*] He was less treacherous than he might have been, wasn't he? [*Pause*] Unless of course the manuscript contained facts that compromised *him*? [*Pause*] Did Mortin ever talk to you about what was in it?

—It was just the first . . . version, that's it, the first version of Mortier's son.

—Do you remember him saying anything about personal details that were very precious to him?

—He could always have put them in again in the other versions . . . how could he have forgotten them if they were as important as all that?

—And suppose the text had been more than a manuscript . . . suppose it had been a . . . sort of . . . file, say, with documents in it?

—I've never thought of that. [*Pause*] But in that case I don't see why documents that were compromising for Johann should have frightened Mortin . . .

—It's you who are forcing us into contradictory theories, when all the time it would probably be perfectly easy for you to tell us what you think.

—I tell you again I don't know.

Interview VI

—I imagine it was Monsieur Cyrille's denying your existence that made you decide to grant us an interview?

—Exactly. We're not living in the Middle Ages now, thank God, and there's nothing shocking in being someone's illegitimate daughter, at least not to me there isn't. Of course Monsieur Cyrille might have said what he did in perfectly good faith, my great-uncle was not obliged to talk about something that he might have thought reflected on my mother. What surprises me though is that Monsieur Cyrille should never have heard of something that was the talk of the whole village.

—You don't know Monsieur Cyrille yourself, don't remember him?

—No. I was too young at the time and my mother and I went to the Argentine after Mortin died.

—How old were you?

—Seven.

—We're told your mother died out there?

—Yes, just ten years ago. That was what made me decide to come back to Europe.

Pause

—Have you seen any of the people you knew as a child that are still alive?

—No. Anyway I can remember hardly anything about my mother's and my uncle's friends . . . my great-uncle if you prefer. As for the orphanage I just have a vague recollection of a sort of nightmare.

—Were you sent to an orphanage?

—Yes. My mother was very conventional. She had to keep up appearances, she said, because of her profession. Appearances, when everybody knew all about it. [*Pause*] But it was the same thing all over again in the Argentine. She suffered all her life because of her irregular situation.

—And didn't you?

—Yes, indirectly, when I was younger. Then . . .

—It didn't prevent you from making your way in the world. You got married when you came back from the Argentine. Your husband comes from round here, doesn't he?

—Yes, the Jumeaus are one of the oldest families in the district. The traditional pattern.

Pause

—You didn't hear the other interviews before the one with Cyrille, so . . .

—Let's stick to Cyrille's mistakes to be going on with. [*Pause*] For example he said that my uncle was never married. That's not true. My mother had a family album, though as a matter of fact I left it in the Argentine, and it had a photo in it of Uncle Alexandre's wedding. His wife was a Mademoiselle Fion, I think, Célestine Fion. My mother used to talk to me about Aunt Célestine. She looked very elegant in the photograph . . . at least I thought so. I adored those fashions when I was a girl.

—So his wife wasn't Mimi, then? Did your mother tell you about her in more detail?

—No. She would just mention Aunt Célestine in the course of conversation. She was very young too when her aunt died. What she remembered most were some cakes that used to be made on special occasions, I don't remember what . . . [*Pause*] and some oldfashioned expression she used to use . . . it's just gone out of my head.

—Do you know anything about . . . about your great-aunt's illness?

—No. But what I heard in the broadcast brought something back to me. I remembered that one day when he was talking about his wife my uncle said something about some medicine and my mother signed to him to be quiet because of me. It suddenly came back to me. If the medicine had been harmless my mother wouldn't have taken any notice. But unfortunately I can't remember what it was. She must have been seriously ill.

—Didn't your mother ever mention it again?

—No. That's what makes me think it must have been something serious. Typical of families, that, isn't it?

—So you don't know what your great-aunt died of?

—No. [*Pause*] But another idea's occurred to me. Perhaps there's a connexion between that medicine and my uncle's attacks of fatigue. I'd never thought of it before.

—Attacks of fatigue, did you say?

—Yes. Often in the middle of the afternoon he'd ask us to go . . . or rather my mother would come and fetch me in from the garden and say we had to go home, Uncle Alexandre was tired . . . [*Pause*] One day as we were going I even saw him through the window, sitting in his chair with his head back and his mouth open, my mother said he was asleep. I've never forgotten the way he sat there.

—What did he die of?

—Some sort of blood-poisoning. My mother never really knew. Or at least she pretended she didn't.

—You didn't see him when he was dying?

—No.

—It was his nephew, your uncle, that inherited the villa, wasn't it?

—Yes. What a business. Your Cyrille must be right about the small house, there was some complication that prevented it from coming to us. My mother spent days at the lawyer's. But she never spoke of it afterwards, and I was too young to take any interest.

—Didn't the name Cyrille mean anything to you when you heard it on the radio?

—No, I didn't remember that name.

—Another, perhaps?

—No.

—You say there were difficulties over who the villa was to go to, too?

—Everyone was careful to keep it all a secret from me, as if I would have understood anything anyway, but I do remember endless sessions between my mother and the lawyer, either in his office or at the house. There was even question of a process being served or something, they sent me into the kitchen and I found a marvellous picture. [*Pause*] It was one of the first coloured postcards.

—What was it of?

—A seaside view. I can see it still.

—Did you read what was on it?

—I hardly knew my alphabet. As soon as my mother saw me with it she snatched it away. [*Pause*] Funny the little things you remember.

Pause

—Strange that you and your mother should never have spoken about all that again afterwards.

—As soon as ever I mentioned the business of the will she used to get so worked up I just didn't pursue it. Even when she was dying she didn't want to talk about it, poor thing. [*Pause*] Not that there was anything to say seeing we hadn't got the villa. What I didn't know was that it was mortgaged.

—It was your Uncle Louis everything went to, wasn't it?

—Pierre. He died a few years later. Five or six years.

—But you did have an Uncle Louis too?

—No, my mother only had the one brother, Uncle Pierre.

—Do you remember someone called Louis that your great-uncle used to have to see him sometimes?

—No.

—And Johann, do you remember him?

—The servant, yes. Vaguely, that is. I remember Noémie the cook better. She was a strange woman, always crying all over the gas-stove. I can remember her black shawl and red hands. And her quince jam. [*Pause*] There was something I wanted to tell you . . . just a moment . . . [*Pause*] Yes. About another house Uncle Alexander had. I heard about it from my husband. It was the family house, where he was born. He let it to a Madame Aubier. I don't know how but she finally managed to get to own it. She was very . . . quick off the mark, apparently. [*Pause*] Anyway these stories of wills and legacies are all alike.

Pause

—And do you remember a Monsieur André?

—No. [*Pause*] The person I remember best is a boy who was a bit gone in the head, Gilles Fontaine, he worked in the carpenter's next door. My mother had forbidden me to go in there with him but of course I went as fast as my legs would carry me. He used to play with me as if we were both children, great booby. He told me horrible stories that made me dream. He must have had an obsession about people getting drowned in the river, according to him it happened or would happen to everyone sooner or later, his boss, his friends in the carpenter's shop, Uncle Alexandre, my mother, Monsieur and Madame Biaule who lived just up the road . . . goodness, now I remember them too. A little old couple. Kept cats. [*Pause*] The macabre thing about it was that poor Fonfon as they called him really was drowned a few years ago.

—People have mentioned drowning to us in connexion with . . . your great-aunt, and even with . . . Alexandre Mortin himself.

—But that's ridiculous! It was just Fonfon's fancy . . .

—Trustworthy people.

—Oh well of course, if you don't consider *me* . . .

—Of course we do, madame, of course we do. What you've been telling us about your childhood throws light over the whole period for us. [*Pause*] Perhaps we ought to spend a bit of time on your opinion of Mortin's work. You must have heard Cyrille say Mortin was telling the story of his own life under the name of Mortier.

—Disgraceful. You might choose better sources of information than waiters in cafés. My grandmother herself knew Daniel Mortier very well when she was in Algeria. He was great friends with my Uncle Alexandre who was there in the army, and before he died he gave my uncle the log-books he'd kept. When Mortin came back to Europe he set himself to write a biography of his friend based on these authentic documents.
Pause

—Your grandmother was in Algeria too, then?

—Yes, she took the opportunity of her brother's being there. It was an unheard-of journey to make in those days. We kept the photographs. [*Pause*] My mother went there twenty years later, too. A sort of pilgrimage . . . [*Pause*]

It was there that I was conceived . . . she came back
bearing her shame, as she put it.

Pause

—And . . . you never met your father?

—No. My mother wouldn't allow the name Mortier to be
mentioned. Yes, I said Mortier. Daniel Mortier's son.
So now you know. It was really to clear that up that I
came. It would be ridiculous to let people go on doubting
the existence of my own father. The biography of
Mortier's son is about him. If my uncle could never
finish it was mainly because my mother was against it.
All his life Mortin was torn between the desire to
publish the book and the fear of upsetting his niece—he
adored her. A . . . tragic dilemma, really. [*Pause*] The
poor thing was incapable of doing anything but re-
produce his memories faithfully, he was completely
without imagination. He looked after his dead friend's
son James as if he were his real father, visited him
regularly in Algeria, paid for his education. Unhappily
for my uncle, James Mortier went into the army too and
was killed up country when he was only twenty-five,
soon after I was born. [*Pause*] His devotion to the
Mortier family made him go on with the second book
even after his niece's disgrace. But she had the last
word. [*Pause*] What infuriates me is that my cousin has
the manuscript and refuses to let it be published.

—Your cousin . . . that would be the son of your Uncle . . .

—Uncle Pierre.

—Of course. [*Pause*] Have you seen the manuscript or does
your cousin refuse to show it to anyone?

—I read it at his house not long ago. It must have been the
fourth or fifth version, but it was still full of crossings-
out and notes in the margin. Mortin must have decided

in the end to change everything out of consideration for my mother, but he couldn't get on with it. I was turned into a boy. I think he even thought of altering the name Mortier to Morier in the end. Childish, wasn't it?

—Were there any details in the manuscript that were left unaltered, that were still true to life?

—Heavens, how should I know, I never even met my father . . . [*Pause*] My mother was turned into an Arab damsel that he met by a fountain. Very poetic. But Mortin kept the fact that my father was married.

—Married?

—That was why he couldn't marry my mother. [*Pause*] There were some very good descriptions of the country. Those were the bits he altered least.

—Do you think the manuscript could be published even in its present state?

—Of course. In facsimile. It would be very interesting . . . from every point of view.

—Did your husband tell you anything else about the family house?

—No, nothing much. [*Pause*] My uncle lived there again for a bit between the time he moved out of the little house and when he moved into the villa. I remember going there with my mother. He lived in a couple of rooms, not very comfortable, the rest was let. The Madame Aubier I told you about had a room on the ground floor and his friend Jacques had all the first floor. The house had been neglected, needed repairs. Especially the kitchen if I remember right. It opened on to a little yard full of second-hand furniture. I remember a wooden horse I used to climb on. I only saw the house and the yard once again. I hardly recognized them.

—Do you remember them mentioning at the time some . . . accident that happened there?

—I don't remember myself, but my husband told me about an explosion, gas, that nearly killed Jacques.

—Your great-uncle wasn't . . . hurt at all?

—He was at the café when it happened. A habit that has its advantages, you see. [*Pause*] My mother told me she'd tried everything to break Uncle Alexandre of that weakness. She brought me up to shun alcohol like the plague. [*Pause*] I can still hear her telling me about one fourteenth of July when they found my uncle and the servant both snoring in a ditch at three o'clock in the morning. She was horrified.

—That seems to establish the fact that he had this . . . weakness. [*Pause*] And you say you have only a vague remembrance of Johann?

—Yes. But my uncle was very attached to him. Up till the time, whenever it was, that he did something he shouldn't have done, I don't remember the details.

—Perhaps your husband could tell you?

—No.

—And who was this Jacques you mentioned?

—He was an orphan, I think. He . . . he'd been brought up by my grandmother, with my mother and uncle. Mother remembered the games they used to play in the yard, the tricks they got up to at school, holidays at the seaside. But all that's of no interest.

—So he was almost a nephew of your great-uncle's.

—If you like.

—That must be how certain confusions have arisen . . . [*Pause*] There were quite a few people in that so-called solitude of Mortin's.

—Aren't you attributing too much importance to these

minor characters? It seems to me you know the essential facts now. Isn't the work what you're really concerned with?

—We wanted to clear up certain aspects of it. But as you say . . . [*Pause*] Just a few last questions. Did you know this Jacques? What's his surname? Have you kept in touch with him? Is he still alive?

—Yes. I've come across him now and again by chance. At least I was told it was him. He . . . he took to drink. The good old tradition. He's become a tramp, more or less, and wanders about the country. People call him Mahu.

Pause

—What about the cook, Noémie?

—Yes, I remember her. I told you.

—Did you know we interviewed her too?

—Noémie? Do you mean to say she's still alive?

—Yes indeed. It was very touching the way she spoke about your great-uncle. [*Pause*] Do you remember anything else about her?

—Well . . .

—Don't be afraid to speak. We can cut.

—The poor thing spent all her life waiting for my uncle to make a declaration. She was practically unhinged. My mother told me the tales she used to spread around about it. She even invented a son she was supposed to have had by Mortin, to try to force him to marry her . . . [*Pause*] I would have laid ten to one she'd already died in the asylum.

—Don't you believe she really did have a son . . . that died in Germany, I think it was?

—Yes, before she went to work for my uncle. But the one she claimed to have had after . . .

Interview VII

—Monsieur Jacques Philippard?

—Call me Mahu. Everyone does.

—Did you acquire this nickname . . . very long ago?

—What?

—Is it many years since people started to call you Mahu?

—You don't think I count them, do you?

—And you live . . . I mean you come from this part of the world, and you've never been away?

—Where would I go?

Pause

—You must have a good many friends.

—No, no friends.

—But . . . you did have . . . I mean you have happy memories, of your childhood for instance?

—Oh that . . .

—You were well brought up, amongst nice people?

—Well brought up, yes . . .

Pause

—Your affections have been thwarted? Your . . . plans haven't met with success?

—Never had any plans. [*Pause*] It's a great honour to be asked to do this . . . this . . . [*Pause*] Excuse me, do you mind if I . . . ? [*Sound of bottle uncorked. Longer pause*] I always carry one with me.

—So I see. [*Pause*] Perhaps you find it painful to talk about your childhood?

—Not painful. Uninteresting, if you see what I mean.

—But you have quite a clear recollection, I suppose . . . of the children you were brought up with, Alexandre Mortin's nephew and niece, and their mother?

—I should think so . . . Odette and Pierre . . . it was a long time ago. [*Pause*] But you know, they . . .

—You don't remember them any too kindly?

—They dropped me . . . got shut of me . . . [*Pause*] I was sent away to school . . . the holidays, we used to see each other during the holidays . . . but then . . .

—You didn't keep up a permanent relationship with your adoptive family?

—It was none of my doing.

—They more or less left you to fend for yourself?

—They did. [*Pause*] No training. What was I supposed to do? [*Pause*] I tried every way to earn a living . . . until the day Alexandre took me in. I called him Alexandre. He was a pal. [*Pause*] If it hadn't been for him . . . [*Pause*] And even so this is how I end up.

—He looked after you until he died?

—Yes. It was out of his hands afterwards.

—So you lived with him for a number of years?

—Twenty . . . they went so quickly . . . it seems like yesterday . . . I'm just an old wreck, but this . . . [*Pause*] This won't grow old.

—You'd rather the heart grew old as well?

—I'd rather everything went together, yes.
Pause

—So Alexandre Mortin was the only member of your family with whom you didn't lose contact?

—I told you I lost contact with all my family, as you call it.

I don't like that word. Alexandre was a pal. [*Pause*] We met one day in a bar. I was thirty. I hardly knew him. [*Pause*] It wasn't because he was my uncle he fished me out of the soup, it was because he was a pal.

—He let one floor of his house to you, didn't he?

—Yes, for nothing. [*Pause*] He never once asked me about work. He knew very well I didn't do a hand's turn. I tried, oh yes, I tried, I'd been all over the place and tried, but when you get to be thirty you can't change your spots . . . [*Pause*] You don't often come across people like him.

—He was your best friend then?

—*He* was *my* best friend. [*Pause*] But that doesn't mean to say I was his . . . he had lots of friends . . . what I mean is you only had to tap him and he was your friend . . . and there were plenty around to do that.

—Did he ask you to his place?

—Yes often.

—Which of his friends did you get on with best?

—He didn't invite us together. He was always alone when I went to see him. He preferred to see just one person at a time.

—Can you recall one of your pleasantest memories of him? Some typical instances of his kindness?

—Well now . . . all my memories of him are pleasant.

—Well, for example, some occasion when you went to see him . . . or when you went out together . . . or . . . I don't know, some meal that you remember, when Mortin said something amusing perhaps . . . or something intriguing . . . [*Pause*] Surely you must remember something of that sort, something that had a particular effect on you?

—Well . . . [*Pause*] What *I* liked best was when we went to pick mushrooms.

—Tell us about it.

—Do you mind if I . . . ? [*Bottle uncorked. Longer pause*] Here we go then. [*Pause*] Towards the end of the summer I used to go and call for him at seven in the morning. He was usually up already and we'd have a cup of coffee together. It was . . . it was . . . I don't know how to describe it . . . [*Pause*] It was the beginning of a day that would have to end . . . I got as much as I could out of every minute . . . I'd have made the coffee last for hours if I could . . . I felt so good when I was with him . . . it was . . . it was peaceful. [*Pause*] He had a way of making me feel comfortable . . . without saying anything, just as if he were alone . . . [*Pause*] Of course he'd known me as a child, he didn't have to stand on ceremony with me . . . but for me . . . it wasn't memories that drew me to him . . . [*Pause*] When you live on your own there's something some people have that makes you . . . that more than anything else makes you . . . I couldn't say what it is . . . [*Pause*] It makes you comfortable. You feel you *are* somebody. You start to talk. You're not afraid of being taken for a . . . you see what I mean. [*Pause*] I've thought a lot about it . . . no-one else ever made me feel like that . . . now there's only the bottle . . . it's not the same . . . but it helps you forget. [*Longer pause*]

—Go on, go on.

—You'll think I'm a windbag but it's so long since I talked about him . . . [*Pause*] When we'd had coffee we started out. I had my satchel and he had his with bread and cheese and a bottle of beaujolais. He always took the

142

best in his cellar. In honour of the mushrooms, he used to say. [*Pause*] We used to take the road to the wood at Le Furet. The mornings were cool already, there was often a mist ... or dew ... or both together nearer the autumn ... at first it would already be hot at nine o'clock ... the Septembers we had in those days ... never seen any like them since ... and not for want of tramping the roads ... [*Pause*] Do you know the wood at Le Furet? [*Pause*] It's all oaks, with a few beeches where it slopes down to the river. You find boletus and beefsteak mushrooms and field mushrooms and cantharellus on the edge of the wood ... in the spring there's morel too but it's hard to find. [*Pause*] There used to be fern growing on the north side but I suppose there's hardly any left since they cut down the trees ... or perhaps there's more ... I don't know.

—Did you get all your mushrooms in the wood?

—No, we went to the forest as well. Grance isn't far, you just have to cross a few fields, follow the main road a little way, go through Crachon village and there you are. [*Pause*] We always used to stop at the Plane Tree café. That would be about nine o'clock. To save the beaujolais. The owner was a man called Monachou, Jean Monachou. His son took over afterwards. [*Pause*] We used to sit outside. Just for a few minutes. Monachou used to give us his white wine, gnat's water. Too early in the morning for the girls, he always used to say. And Mortin always used to say the better the hour the better the deed. Every time. For years. [*Pause*] I liked that. Something that stays the same. Always repeating the same thing. Mortin said one day that that was why I'd never achieve anything, like him. He was convinced he was a complete failure. [*Pause*] I've thought about that too . . . he didn't just say it for effect, he really believed it . . . and he wrote books . . . whereas I . . . it's all very well for me to call myself a failure but what have I ever produced?

—He said it out of modesty.

—He wasn't happy. I suppose modesty can be some sort of help? He was convinced he was the lowest of the low. The times we've groused together.

—He wasn't always cheerful then?

—God no. But he never kept anything back, and we always used to end up laughing.

—Did he talk to you about his work?

—Mostly he just used to tell me he couldn't make any headway with it. I wasn't clever enough to discuss it.
Pause

—Well, to get back to the mushrooms.

—Do you mind if . . . ? [*Bottle uncorked. Longer pause*] We got to the forest along a sunken lane called the Corridor. The beeches were all golden over our heads. Mortin used to say it was oriental. It reminded him of something in North Africa. We used to follow the Corridor as far as the clearing . . . or else turn to the left along the path leading north. There was St. George's mushroom all over the place and saffron milk-cap and russula . . . farther in there were boletus again, ruddy warty caps and blewits . . . [*Pause*] You find parasols and lawyer's wig more in the fields, and pholiota . . . I often confuse the names these days . . . I still dream about them . . . [*Pause*] One day he found a boletus that wasn't in his

book. He went all the way into town the next day to try to find out about it. No-one had ever heard of it. He called it a philippard to please me. We never found another. [*Pause*] About eleven we used to sit down for a bite. There are some rocks to the east of the gully . . . our feet used to be quite wet. The cheese tasted of the cloth it was wrapped in . . . and the beaujolais was warm . . . [*Pause*] I used to think again if only it could last . . . I couldn't do without it any more . . . [*Pause*] He didn't say anything, just munched his cheese and stared at the gully . . . his hat had gone all grey . . . it was a brown felt from before the first war . . . we handed the bottle backwards and forwards . . . we had to make room in his satchel for more mushrooms . . . we used to throw the empty bottle into the gully . . . I can still hear the sound . . . [*Pause*] Mademoiselle Ariane met us there one day when she was out collecting mushrooms. She asked us up to the house to sample her beaujolais. We went back with her. The first and last time I set foot there. She laughed at me because I was so awkward. [*Pause*] You know I think it might have been her who first called me Mahu . . . that was the sort of thing she used to do . . .
—Who was Mademoiselle Ariane?
—The owner of Bonne-Mesure. She's been dead a long time. Nearly the whole forest belonged to her. She used to let Mortin pick mushrooms on her land . . . a funny woman, looked like a farmer's wife . . . huge shawl and little eyes like a mouse and white hair all over the place. [*Pause*] We drank quite a lot of her beaujolais . . . it wasn't any better than ours but drinking it there like that . . . she told us stories about her family, grand-

K

fathers, grandmothers, right back to the Crusades . . . there was a servant hanging about outside waiting for us to go, he was afraid she might go too far . . . she had a reputation for being a bit free . . . but I didn't notice anything out of the way the day we were there . . . or perhaps she hadn't taken to us enough . . . [*Pause*] Mademoiselle Ariane . . . [*Pause*] She had a kite like a . . . sorry. [*Pause*] What was I saying . . . [*Pause*] The bread and cheese . . . Mortin's hat . . . one day he lost it in the forest, we went back and looked everywhere for it, he wouldn't give up, in the end we found it in Dead Man's Dell . . . someone supposed to have hung himself . . . some people say Judas, others say Vaoua the witch . . . she used to get up to tricks with all the young men . . . it's written down somewhere . . . some book, I don't remember the title, Mortin showed it to me . . . [*Pause*] The books he'd read . . . too many he said . . . he couldn't finish his own . . . [*Pause*] It was sad in a way, it used to depress him . . . but if he had finished it he wouldn't have been the same . . . I've thought about it . . . he wouldn't have had time to . . . he'd have become I don't know . . . a professor or something . . . lectures and God knows what . . . no more mushrooms, no more beaujolais . . . do you mind . . . ? [*Bottle uncorked. Longer pause*] There's life for you, no understanding it . . . what it's best to be . . . what it's best not . . . if I'd been him I wouldn't have regretted anything . . . myself, I regret . . . I regret not having . . . if I'd been him I wouldn't have become what I have become . . . I'd have regretted not having . . . do you mind . . . ?

—Not too much, Monsieur Mahu, not too much now.

Tell us some more about your friend.

—My friend, you're right there . . . what do you want me
to say . . . it's not the same thing . . . what you say and
what you do . . . [*Pause*] You can't talk about it . . . [*Pause*]
If she hadn't died too she'd have let me live in her
barn . . . great big barn full to bursting . . . [*Pause*] Go
back to the dell in the morning . . . he didn't talk any
more, didn't look any more . . . even the boletus that he
christened philippard . . . my satchel full . . . Karas might
have died . . . what would they have said . . .

—We're talking about Mortin, tell us about Mortin, not
Karas.

—He was called Karas . . . the Philippards adopted him
when he was three . . . that made another cousin of that
name . . . little fair chap, in trade . . . they called him
Carabas . . . he was all right on beaujolais but when it
came to mushrooms . . . didn't like them, Carabas
didn't . . .

—You're getting mixed up. Too much beaujolais. [*Pause*]
So your name was Karas before you were adopted?

—What . . . how . . . yes, Karas . . . Mortin called him
Carabas . . . only Mortin . . . the others called him Mahu
. . . always nicknames . . . little fair chap they said . . . in
trade, remember . . . tried everything, did all he could
. . . life . . . what is it . . . adopted . . . never alter . . .
everyone the same . . . people . . . if they only knew . . .
nothing . . . came to nothing . . .

—Come now, Monsieur Mahu, make an effort. [*Pause*] So
Mortin's niece and nephew were called Philippard,
Odette and Pierre Philippard . . . [*Pause*] That's your
name too, isn't it? [*Pause*] So Mortin became your uncle

when you were adopted? [*Pause*] Or did people just
call you Philippard for convenience? [*Pause*] Were you
legally adopted?
—Adopted . . . disadopted . . . who . . . who's going to . . .
what he would have done if I . . . what he would have
done . . .

Interview VIII

—. . . going to ask Monsieur Latirail, primary school master and . . .

—Secondary.

—Excuse me, secondary school master and contributor to the *Fantomiard*, the local newspaper, if he'll be good enough to begin by clearing up a point that has been left . . . unresolved . . . [*Pause*] Monsieur Latirail, do you know whether or not Jacques Karas, otherwise known as Philippard, otherwise known as Mahu, was legally adopted by Madame Philippard, Alexandre Mortin's sister, in other words if Philippard was his real name?

—He was never adopted, I consulted the records at the town hall. His real name is still Karas. [*Pause*] It's true he was brought up by the Philippards but that doesn't make him one himself. Jacques must be an assumed name too. His parents were gipsies I remember seeing about when I was a child. As for Mahu that's just a nickname.

—Did you know the Philippards well?

—We were neighbours for years. I used to play with Pierre and Odette and Jacques as they called him.

—Have you kept in touch with them?

—No. [*Pause*] Anyway they're all dead.

—What about Madame Jumeau?

—Yes, I suppose in a way she's . . . but I don't know the lady.

—And Pierre's son. [*Pause*] And did you know Alexandre Mortin?

—Certainly I did. [*Pause*] That's to say . . . he was a gentleman and we were only working-class . . . he didn't speak to just anyone. [*Pause*] I was in touch with him professionally once or twice in connexion with . . . with his work, as they call it. An author in our own village, that was something. I made a close study of his work. I wrote several critical articles on it in our local paper while Mortin was still alive . . . [*Pause*] Out of a sort of cowardice I passed over a certain . . . weakness in the work . . . or rather in the author, to put it mildly.

—Would you mind explaining?

—Well . . . actually, the book isn't by him at all. Now the cat's out of the bag. I shall never stop reproaching myself for not having dared to speak out at the time. I was young and inexperienced . . . a bit of a careerist too if you like. I thought I'd better watch my step with a writer, and a local one at that. [*Pause*] Mortin was a notability, the council would have been down on me like a ton of bricks, and I had my living to make, had to try to get a job as a schoolmaster . . . you know how it is. [*Pause*] The book about Mortier is really *by* Mortier. I served under Captain Daniel Mortier in Algeria. I was his batman. I was with him when he died, he was stabbed with a dagger. He used to confide in me and I know all about him and the so-called friendship with Mortin. [*Pause*] They'd met in Algiers. Mortin was fascinated by the captain's literary talent. He used to write down all his thoughts in his logbook, I knew them by heart. A masterpiece. [*Pause*] He had the unfortunate idea, the fatal idea, of handing his notes over to Mortin. He'd begged to be allowed to read them. When the captain died Mortin claimed he'd been given them as trustee. As evidence he quoted the letter in which Mortier merely said he was letting him have the notes, without actually saying anything specific. [*Pause*] I did everything I could to get them back, I got Madame Mortier to intervene but she wasn't really interested. Mortin published what Mortier had written as his, without even a preface referring to the notebooks. Nearly all of it had been copied out word for word. All the changes were for the worse.

—And . . . didn't you ever think of writing an article to establish the truth?

—I did write one after Mortin's death. I couldn't even get the local paper, the paper I write for, to print it. The editor refused. I sent it to a review and no-one took the slightest notice of it. [*Pause*] I seize this belated opportunity to denounce the book as a fraud, and to proclaim from the housetops . . .

—Now, Monsieur Latirail, don't let's get carried away. We don't dispute what you say, but you know when it comes to literary matters . . . especially as you're the only person who takes this . . . this attitude.

—For the very good reason that I'm the only one who knew the notebooks. But it's disgusting that . . .

—Perhaps you should have tried to prevent this misunderstanding at the time the book was published . . .

—I've told you why I didn't.

—Well the most sensible thing to do now is accept the facts as they are and tell us calmly all you know about the notebooks and the relations between Mortier and Mortin. [*Pause*] Why did you say their so-called friendship?

—Because it didn't exist. Mortier saw through Mortin from the word go. He was worldly, a snob. But in a way he flattered him and . . . well, flattery is always . . . [*Pause*] But that didn't prevent Mortier from telling me what he thought of him. Sometimes he could hardly bear all his attentions. But the captain was a magnanimous man and trusted him. He didn't feel justified in turning him out . . . took pity on him, to tell the truth. [*Pause*] And that was how Mortin came to get hold of the notebooks. I told Mortier straight away I thought it was unwise, but he said it didn't matter. It seemed ludicrous to him that anyone should attach any importance to his notes . . . [*Pause*] That was just another proof of his genius . . .

—So the notebooks remained in Mortin's possession?

—Yes. Until they disappeared.

—Disappeared?

—They were destroyed. [*Pause*] Johann, the man who used to be Mortin's servant, had a great deal of influence over him. Mortin never moved a finger without consulting him. Even when it was a question of his work. Apparently he was in the habit or reading every page to him as it was written . . .

—How do you know?

—Noémie told me. She used to be the cook.

—She told us she didn't work for Mortin at the same time as Johann.

—Johann used to go and see Mortin still for a long time

after he stopped working for him. They went on with
the book about Mortier's son together. [*Pause*] One
evening they had a violent quarrel . . . Johann threatened
him . . . with a knife, apparently. He went off with the
notebooks. And destroyed them the same night. Threw
them down the well in the churchyard . . . [*Pause*]
Mademoiselle Meyer who lived nearby saw him with
her own eyes.

—How did she know it was the notebooks?

—There could be no doubt about it. They were bound in
white morocco. Three volumes.

—And knowing their value didn't you try . . . didn't you
at least try to fish them out again?

—I didn't know about it till ten years later.
  Pause

—You were speaking of alterations in the text. Can you
tell us what parts were altered? Where there many of
them?

—All the beginning is false for a start. Mortier wasn't born
in the rue de Lamoricière, it was the rue Bugeaud, in
Algiers. His mother was a Ramblaz from Dijon, not
a Rambat. His father was never a chief inspector of
taxes, he was just an ordinary inspector. His parents had
three children not two. The third was a daughter who
died when she was five. Daniel didn't choose to go in
the army, his father made him. He told me himself how
much he regretted it. [*Pause*] As to the family house, there
never was one. The only house he could remember was
one they'd rented on the coast for two years from 1918
to 1920, an uncomfortable hole without the slightest
resemblance to the house described on page 22.

—You know the text very well.

—On page 35 there's the description Mortier wrote of Bourkika. The name has been changed to Birtouta, a completely different place. Birtouta is ten miles south of Algiers whereas Bourkika is getting on for fifty miles to the south-west, and the vegetation . . .

—We only need the main points . . . such as whether the picture the book gives of Mortier himself is modified at all . . .

—Entirely altered, distorted into a middle-class nonentity like Mortin himself, a complete travesty . . . [*Pause*] As for the style of the linking passages, the less said about them the better. On page 56 . . .

—Is all this included in your most recent article?

—Yes. It's at your disposal.

Pause

—Perhaps it would be best to get back to Mortin . . . to your recollections of his family. [*Pause*] You knew Odette Philippard well when she was a girl.

—Yes.

—Her mother as well?

—Mortin's sister, yes. She was a widow. She got married again to an American and went over there to live. California, I think. Pierre was twenty and Odette was eighteen. They stayed behind to finish their studies.

—Did you go on seeing them after their mother went away?

—No. We didn't live near each other any more and I didn't like the way they started to go on.

—But you knew about the affair between Odette and Mortier's son? [*Pause*] Didn't you?

—I didn't wish to have anything to do with that sort of . . .

—Speak out. Don't be afraid.

—Well, if you insist . . . [*Pause*] That fairy-story about Mortier's son is just eyewash. The most squalid middle-class eyewash. [*Pause*] Odette slept with her uncle. Yes. When she went to Algiers to stay with the Mortiers, who were the only people they knew there, it was just to save appearances. She was pregnant already. She came back here to have the baby, as she and her lover had arranged. Her daughter Germaine, Madame Jumeau, is Mortin's daughter. [*Pause*] The reason why they weren't his heirs was that they refused the inheritance. Mortin was up to his eyes in debt. It was Pierre who paid everything off. The mother and daughter went to the Argentine when the scandal broke, after Mortin's death. A disgusting story . . .

—Why should Madame Jumeau, who seems to have so little regard for convention, say she's James Mortier's daughter and not Mortin's? Especially when Mortin's such a famous writer . . .

—Just more eyewash, just another middle-class reaction. I don't see what she gets out of it. But it's in line with the whole family policy, the object of which is to whitewash Mortin's memory. [*Pause*] Very subtle to put on these advanced airs. Makes the whole thing look more convincing.

—But why should she pick on James Mortier and not someone completely unknown?

—They must have got tangled up in their own lies while Mortin was still alive. [*Pause*] But do you notice how that

sort of attitude is proof against every disillusion?
Mortin behaved abominably, he put his own daughter
into an orphanage and didn't leave her a penny, but she
still goes on denying it all. [*Pause*] And she thinks that by
passing herself off as Mortier's daughter she whips up
the interest in her father's book.
Pause
—Where do you get all your information?
—Where do I get my information? I'm only repeating what
everyone knows. What everyone used to know, anyhow.
[*Pause*] What stands out a mile is that everyone con-
nected with Mortin, closely or otherwise, turned a blind
eye. All middle-class nonentities, whether they were
servants or not.
—And . . . how old was Mortin when he . . . when the . . .
—When he made Odette pregnant? Fifty-three. She was
thirty.
Pause
—Madame Jumeau may say what she does in perfectly
good faith. Her mother may simply have hidden the
truth from her.
—And do you mean to say she wouldn't have heard any
rumours when she came back from America? Impossible.
Pause
—It's also somewhat . . . difficult to believe that out of all
the people we've interviewed so far not a single one
has hinted at this matter . . . and that merely out of con-
siderations of propriety.
—Believe it or not as you like. [*Pause*] Perhaps the truth is
best known outside the charmed circle. None so deaf
as those who will not hear.

Pause

—To sum up, Monsieur Latirail, you judge the work very severely. You say the original sources ought at least to have been indicated, and that Alexandre Mortin hadn't enough talent to present the material adequately in the form of a biography.

—Exactly. I'd go even further on the subject of Mortin's . . . capacities. I'd say it is not impossible that Mortier's notes were collated and transcribed by Johann. [*Pause*] And that the second book, the one that remained in manuscript, was written entirely by him. [*Pause*] I know him slightly. Or rather I did. [*Pause*] I used to go to the Swan. Johann went there too. He was suspicious of me. But when he'd had a few he wasn't so guarded. I can put two and two togther by taking the hints he let slip and comparing them with what Noémie said. [*Pause*] The fact that he destroyed Mortier's notebooks after the first book was published doesn't invalidate what I say. When he stopped working for Mortin he deprived him both of his original sources, which judging by the size of the notebooks must have been far from exhausted, and of his, Johann's, own talent, if that is the word. It was a characteristic stroke, intended to put paid to all Mortin's literary ambitions. And in fact it succeeded. Mortin never managed to write the second book.

—There could have been other reasons for that, such as the one Madame Jumeau suggested. The wish not to upset his niece . . .

—But he was doing her a service in making the child out to be Mortier's instead of his own.

—In any case it would only be turning the knife in the

wound. It was to both their advantages to let people forget the whole thing.

—An author's vanity doesn't stop to consider such things.

—You yourself have accused Mortin of being middle-class and conventional.

—I...I...[*Pause*] And what if I proved to you that Johann did write?

—He told us that himself. A very touching kind of memoir about Mortin's sayings and doings. But he could never get it down properly, and it was his notes for this memoir, not Mortier's notebooks, that he threw down the well.

—That's not true.

—Prove it.

—Here.

Longer pause

—What are these papers?

—Johann's notes. [*Longer pause. Sound of pages turned*] You can see the different versions.

—What is there to prove that this . . .

—Was written by Johann? Look at it, read it . . .

Pause. Sound of pages again

—It would only be fair for you to tell us where you got these papers from.

—Just stick to the fact that they're there. You wouldn't be satisfied with any explanation. Whatever I said would only start up more arguments. You've got the proof in your hands.

Notes

Just note, simply note down, without stopping I lose the thread, an old story I need to get it over with, I've only got this notebook but that should be enough with a bit of effort, these things I thought them at the time no reason why they should have gone, a bit of effort and I'll find them somewhere, here first page I start again I've put down melancholy hibernation . . .

Melancholy hibernation first word noted down that Monday of the last week, I hesitated a long time over the exact meaning and when I decided ᴜ write it down I looked it up in the dictionary. It said winter torpor or sleep, that's it, torpor of certain animals, he said it of himself a running down a sort of abandon, meaning he was going to get drowsy go to sleep or slow down as he did every year when winter was coming he slept more he worked less but that year that last Monday he said melancholy because something had just happened, a sorrow he'd had the old great sorrow, a telegram sister passed away after so many years so far away, not that he really loved her but it was the last link as if the memory of what he used to be no longer existed after that day, as if seeing sister passed away he who'd been able to carry on with the idea she was still there to sustain him or make him remember the old days and let him still be there himself in spite of all the trouble, as if seeing that he wasn't there any more, he didn't say it but I knew that must be it because I myself . . .

That Monday as usual I went to wake him at eight, he got up came down showed me the telegram I didn't know anything about it till then, I said how awful or how sad, he didn't say anything, I served the coffee he didn't look at me I tried to think of something to say I couldn't then he picked up the telegram and said something like all life long you keep trying to write it down inside yourself and when it happens to you you hardly recognize it, I understood very well because I myself . . .

It struck me or perhaps later on not at the time, later on thinking about it struck me that what you understand best is what's most difficult to say. There are probably various ways of understanding and mine's a bad one it can't be expressed, a bad one yes the way that hurts the most because you can't say anything, I've thought about it for years, bad but not mistaken, you couldn't be wrong your whole life long about what happens to us it's not possible . . .

He drank his coffee cold I still trying to think of something to say he looking out of the window, he picked up the telegram again got up went and sat down as usual at his desk on the other side of the room, put the telegram in the left-hand drawer where he kept letters, bills, photographs I used to tell him to burn them, why poison himself fermenting bygones as he put it, he wanted to it helped him in his work apparently first on Mortier, then on the son as if his disappointments his regrets his unfinished business what shall I say . . . his emotional failures were the source of all truth, his and other people's, truth in general, as if by drawing on them one could speak about anything whatever. At least that's how I explain his mixing up what happened to him with what happened to Mortier . . .

He put the telegram in the drawer, stayed there thinking while I did the housework and got the lunch ready, the door was open that's when I heard him saying over and over melancholy hibernation I wrote it down in my notebook straight away, he said it several times in just under an hour, through the window I could see the sad late autumn scene, the grass the bed of little chrysanthemums we'd planted that year they were fading, the kitchen-garden with the sorrel border, the last of the leeks, the fountain, the oaks . . .

Our relations were deteriorating for various reasons and I could foresee the time when I should have to stop coming, he'd always been difficult to get on with but for some time it had been getting worse, we didn't talk as we used to he was going silent, often he didn't answer when I spoke, that's the worst, words never killed anybody but silence destroys you inch by inch the surest way not only the one who's waiting listening but also the one who won't speak. When I realized he was turning in on himself I did everything I could to stop it, I talked all the time clumsily perhaps but it seemed better than nothing, when he was impatient I tried not to mind, I said to myself what does it matter if he does jump down my throat, what ought to be prevented I could feel it coming . . .

When we first knew each other he still lived with his mother she died soon after he never got over it, stubborn woman she was he never contradicted her, it was from her because of her he had this artificial side to him this placid appearance when really all the time his nerves were on edge, she didn't like anything he liked or anything he did in a nutshell she didn't like him, always fishing for compliments on her cooking or her housekeeping or complaining, she could hardly stand bowels didn't work insomnia she slept like a log, I didn't shed many tears over her and she could hardly bear the sight of me told God knows what tales about me, no I didn't shed many tears over her . . .

So that Monday he must have gone on daydreaming while I got on with the work but when I took him his cup of tea at about eleven he'd gone back to his manuscript and had his pen in his hand though he wasn't writing, the left-hand drawer was open again he must have re-read the telegram or been looking at his photographs, I didn't like to say anything and went back to the kitchen thinking it won't last he'll wallow in his grief for one or two days I know that's how it takes him but it'll buck him up in the end, after all the death of a sister is more stimulating than raw leeks or the sound of the electric saw next door. I read a few lines of Vauvenargues, he'd put me on to him, a sensitive writer he's made me understand some things but never brought me any consolation . . .

Then I cooked the chops we had chops every Monday and made a salad of beetroot and lamb's-lettuce and started the coffee and served the lunch at twelve o'clock. He didn't keep me waiting the times before he'd gone on and finished his paragraph and nothing I could do but heat everything up again, even if I asked him was he sure he'd finished sure I could really dish up he'd say yes and then not come, but that day he almost ran to the table and straight away he asked wasn't there a bottle of Pommard left. He never used to drink in the middle of the day it made him go to sleep over his work, I said I'll go and look but all the time I knew there wasn't any left we'd finished the last one with his niece the last time she came, so I go to the cellar and find a bottle of rosé from the Magasins-Prix better than nothing, I fetch it up and he makes the most awful scene, never anything to be found in this rotten hole, I neglect all the work on the pretext I'm educated educated he couldn't say it often enough, it must have been me drank the Pommard, the one day he has a right to some solace, to cut a long story short he hadn't talked so much for months. I merely said in the first place after all I'm not your servant, and in the second let me remind you we finished the last bottle with your niece, and finally I'd be glad if you'd measure your words that started him off again, measure my words measure my words you keep dinning it into me I won't speak and now I've got to measure my words, those are my words if you want to know. I went out of the room and ate my chop on my own in the kitchen, I didn't say anything when I served the coffee I had mine with him, he'd calmed down he was looking out of the window the abscess had burst . . .

His niece was in her thirties the daughter of the sister who'd just died, a spinster a schoolteacher sallow complexion and bad teeth, she came to see him every month, we didn't get on she wouldn't even deign to say good-morning to me that bothered Mortin a lot at first but he was glad of it towards the end. I knew she came for what she could get she was sure her uncle was well off, as she was the only heir she made up to him didn't want to risk seeing everything go either to me at first at the time when he and I were friends, or afterwards to one of the people he knew after his mother died, she couldn't bear the idea kept writing to her own mother Mortin's sister that is to tell her what was going on and try to separate him from the other person, called on even distant cousins and friends to rally round as if they cared . . .

After lunch I raked the path I thought the niece would come over to mourn the sister here, no question of her going to California for that and lo and behold she was at it again the next day she telephoned first, then I went in to make the tea, usual routine. It was then for no particular reason because after all our estrangement had started a long time before that I suddenly felt the void, the void I can't call it anything else. I wasn't the person I used to be any more, I'd taken refuge somewhere else, the idea I'd built up of our friendship, taken refuge in something that no longer existed, suddenly I'd been alone in the kitchen a long time. He couldn't bear me in the living-room, as soon as meals were over I had to disappear, I did it willingly to help his work, to contribute something to our relationship but it was only a pretence now, the whole machinery was falling to pieces. To contribute something by not being there, what sorrow . . .

His sister's death didn't make things any better but I didn't have the heart to say anything any more, he must have puzzled over the telegram a long time how to word it then he put it off till the next day he'd do it with his niece, there were problems the sister had re-married the niece was a daughter by her first marriage didn't get on either with her stepfather or her half-brothers and sisters, the telegram had to be neither one thing nor the other polite on the surface but hinting plainly the niece was quite prepared to go over if there were any complications about the will the same sort of thing was quite likely in store for him, to cut a long story short he started to read a magazine, I could hear him drumming on the arms of the chair and sighing . . .

In the evening I started to do the potatoes for dinner, he went for a walk round the garden it was getting dark it had started to rain, I told him to put on his raincoat he didn't, he must have stood up under the roof of the hen-house to keep out of the wet. I couldn't make up my mind whether to open a tin of crab or not, ought I to make up for the disappointment over the bottle of Pommard or would it be better just to forget it, in the end I opened it and made a mayonnaise, a queer idea came into my head connecting funerals and mayonnaise no explaining these things and I started to laugh to myself just nerves and of course he had to come in at that precise moment when he saw me laughing he scowled and banged the door I was sorry about the crab then but it was too late he was bound to have seen it on the table. Soon after that I heard him opening the bottle of port he was trying to calm himself down good sign that, I took the opportunity for a bit of play-acting and went to suggest a glass of port as an apéritif I started to speak before I got inside the room so I could look surprised that he'd had the same idea, that sort of coincidence generally helps to smooth things over . . .

Next day Tuesday I got the lunch ready early, escalopes salad fried potatoes the niece would have a good guzzle, and a cheese soufflé to start with. About ten I wanted to lay the table so as not to have to do it at the last minute but Mortin said I was disturbing him he'd lay it himself when he'd finished, and by the way he said perhaps you wouldn't mind not joining us today we've got family business to discuss. So for the first time I was relegated to the kitchen, it was almost better in a way I couldn't stick the niece turning up her nose at me but it was the end all right . . .

I walked down to the carpenter's shop to take my mind off there was a workman there simple sort of a chap he was glad to talk to me no need to keep asking myself was I boring him, Fonfon he was called, his name was Fontaine, Gilles, he told me his mother had nearly died of an instruction he meant obstruction she was cured by a miracle, we talked about illnesses all his all mine all those in the village it's an inexhaustible subject, but the great malady that brought us together at that moment we didn't mention that it gnawed at my heart and his too though he didn't know it, the terrible loneliness of the outcast and the inconsolable . . .

I went back to the house I asked Mortin what did he want me to do would he serve the meal himself or should I, was the niece not to see me, he told me I was to serve but not keep putting my oar in all the time I got on his nerves always talking, so I waited till she arrived to put my soufflé in the oven. She came at twelve on a bicycle all in black with a crape band round her neck, she propped her bike up against the plane-tree and when she saw me she said Oh you where's my uncle, I'd got a little speech of condolence ready in case but I didn't need it, she put on a grief-stricken expression and disappeared into the living-room and when she saw Mortin she said what not in mourning, Mortin said you know I never go out if I go into the village I'll put on my black suit. She said she'd been that morning to buy her hat she'd had to beat them down it was a bargain must observe the proprieties so what are we going to do. Mortin said there isn't anything to do except write the telegram we'll see about that after lunch and put an announcement in the paper, we must send cards she said I inquired so much a dozen in copper-plate very distinguished. Mortin wouldn't agree straight away they didn't know very many people it was a needless expense, she was outraged, my pupils' parents and the archaeological society whatever should we look like, in the end he said he'd pay for it and poured out the port . . .

In the afternoon I worked in the garden I weeded the vegetables and sat in the sun dreaming in the corner where the aromatic herbs grew, there were all sorts. Laurel from Italy, thyme from Provence, rosemary we bought from the man who sold birds, mint we got from a field near a stream where the boys used to blow up frogs, sage, savory, fennel two or three slips, chervil, celery, tarragon, horse-radish, chives, marjoram, angelica . . .

I loved it that corner I shall never see it again it made me long for an ideal garden where you never got tired, full of good smells and kept promises . . .

I went in it was getting dark . . .

The Hypothesis

For Jean Martin

A sparsely furnished room. On the right, bookshelves. At the back a small stove standing out against a dazzling white wall. To the left a table and an armchair. Mortin sits in the chair; he is wearing a dress suit. Very tall, very gaunt, a wild look in his eye. He tries to repeat a speech by heart to an imaginary audience, though the text is there in front of him. Also on the table is a jug of water and a glass.

For the most part Mortin speaks as if by rote, ignoring the inflections, pauses and stresses the meaning would seem to dictate. He often stops, hesitates, and refers to the text. Now and then there are passages he is more confident of, and these he emphasises with variations of tone and histrionic gestures.

He speaks fairly fast.

MORTIN: In a sense clearly one might say the manuscript is at the bottom of a well but then it couldn't be at our place because there wouldn't be any more wells there so at some time or another the author would have had to go somewhere else even if only for a very short while taking the manuscript with him but what for? On the one hand no-one seems to remember ever having seen him go anywhere on the other hand everyone who had more than a nodding acquaintance with him seems to maintain that his manuscript was glued to his desk and that he couldn't work anywhere else. [*Pause*] So we should have to allow in order not to let the last chance slip through our fingers that he did go away for say one or two days with his manuscript that no-one saw him go and that he came back in the same way a hypothesis of no interest since everyone who had more than a nodding acquaintance with him is supposed to have seen his manuscript glued down to his desk right up to the last but in a sense the hypothesis could save the whole situation. [*Pause*] According to which the manuscript then would have gone down the drain and all he'd put in it getting up in the middle of the night not eating any more ears always on the stretch so to speak not only for words and sounds but also for the most ineffable silences and God knows there would be plenty of those . . . would have have been plenty of those . . . [*Pause*] ineffable silences and God knows there would have have been plenty of those, determining circumstances which in view of their repercussions or rather consequences beyond the conditional might pass for causes of a situation such that without these circumstances this situation would not exist in the present and a whole lot of other circumstances existing in the present without which this entirely conditional situation would not have . . . without which this situation would not have . . . [*He is stuck. Pause. He refers to the text. Looks up.*] without which this situation would be in the present instead of the conditional hence stripped scraped down to the bone non-existent so it is clear that the well the improbable well at someone else's place would be a means of getting from this situation let's leave it vague to another and deriving from it et cetera I abbreviate in the case in question because there would be wells there whereas here not, would finally tend therefore to establish that the absence of any equivalent in other words the exceptional nature of the case would be the only element not perfectly established in other words real. [*Pause. He takes his handkerchief out of his pocket and blows his nose. Pause. Refers to text, etc.*] Now the hypothesis having been admitted of the manuscript at the bottom of the well and the latter not being immediately at hand the author would have had to go somewhere else hence break habits which neither the neighbours nor those who had more than a nodding acquaintance with him could have suspected it was possible to break equally because of first of all the author's stay-at-home disposition, second his lack of imagination, third his dislike of performing any action that might give rise to comment, fourth the fact that without his manuscript he would have been to all intents and purposes non-existent, fifth the difficulty he'd have had seeing he was so lazy in detaching the said manuscript which according to those who had more than a nodding acquaintance with him only an expert at the very least could have torn off that desk left corner by the window, sixth the unlikelihood even if the said manuscript were detached of the author's going away anywhere with it which would imply he intended to work on it somewhere other than at his own desk which is simply unthinkable, as we were saying in spite of all the above reasons which one would have expected to act as a powerful deterrent the picture that's where we inevitably end up of the author leaning over this well and throwing his manuscript down it instead of himself this picture seems to impose itself and immediately require if the hypothesis is to stand to be if not developed at least left unchallenged which would present in addition to the above circumstances representing difficulties here and reasons there an almost insurmountable obstacle which we should nevertheless be prepared to surmount or abolish cost us what it might. [*Pause. He drums his fingers on the table.*] Or abolish costs us what it might. [*Pause. Consults text, etc.*] It should also be said that the glued down manuscript might be a replica of the first a hypothesis another hypothesis involving the first one and thus implying not only the going away in the middle of the night the throwing in the water the coming back alone but also the deception and the necessity for the deception. [*Pause*] Why should the author who would seem to have devoted himself to his writing in conditions of the utmost security have felt the need to throw dust in people's eyes thus giving himself the trouble of copying it all out again, could his safety be only apparent, could he have had a feeling he was surrounded by enemies, or if not by enemies by suspicion, what could he have been suspected of, could this suspicion have been justified, or would it not rather have been some conspiracy malice jealousy fear terror danger, would it be reasonable to put forward danger as a hypothesis, danger to whom, an isolated group society which would imply either that not all those who had more than a nodding acquaintance with him were his friends or that there were other people too unknown people who not only do not appear in any account of the author's doings but who this is the point must have without the knowledge of the said author in view of his stay-at-home and taciturn disposition introduced themselves into his house in order to find out find out what, glued down manuscript replica of the first, previous work on the latter, copying out of the former, clues to the reasons for it all what all, the author's doubts, anxiety troubled sleep . . . troubled sleep . . . [*A cinematic projection of Mortin's face, twice life-size, appears on the wall at the back. Very clear. Ten seconds. Mortin notices it, brushes his hand over his eyes. The face disappears. Pause. Mortin consults the text, etc.*] Anxiety troubled sleep because it must be assumed as a constant that the glued down one was not just a sham all hypotheses break down else all reality reality of what, of the facts which without this hypothesis not only could not be as they are but would not neither there nor here at our place where the absence of the well alone would have given rise to it would have created a shadow of doubt establishing so to speak the author at his desk who could not have written subsequently what without the complicity of those who had more than a nodding acquaintance with him supposing them to be his friends he could not have known about himself being no more than a hypothesis. [*Pause. He stands up and leans his hands on the table.*] The author the author where is the author. [*Pause*] It is to `e supposed finally that in view of the lack of evidence against the hypothesis of the well the author must necessarily have gone to it granted the difficulty the simple difficulty of supposing that at a certain moment I emphasise this the idea should have occurred but to whom of a possible connexion between this lack or rather insufficiency and the fact that at that moment a certain uneasiness would more noticeably but for whom have tended to take shape either literary or merely psychological, in this connexion to have no grounds for supposing anything at all doesn't seem any more to be desired . . . doesn't seem any more to be desired. [*He is stuck. Pause. Consults text. etc.*] Doesn't seem to be any more to be desired than the contrary it being impossible for the uneasiness in question to arise out of anything but an apparently human complex unless we were to delve into considerations fortunately not indispensable a certain complex let's leave it vague including an infinite number of possibles taken here in the sense of phenomena a postulate even more baffling than the hypothesis since while not actually existing at all they would be pre-existent to it. [*Pause*] That would puzzle us . . . [*Pause*] puzzle us the author at his desk writing as if he were the supposed author whom before the hypothesis of the well and without prejudice he would have in fact consigned either directly on to the manuscript glued to the desk or on to a draft which without prejudice his neighbours or relations would have known about facts then not forgotten gestures set down and words hardly significant enough to deserve recording the author . . . the author where's the author . . . [*He walks round the desk and over to the bookshelves. Spends some time looking for a book he can't find. Gesture of impatience. Pause. Turns towards audience.*] hardly significant enough to deserve recording. The author new hypothesis would have found himself placed in circumstances which without the hypothesis of the well neither he nor the real author nor you nor I nor anyone else could ever have

dreamed of circumstances I repeat problematical circumstances but it would be best then to accept them it
would get us on a lot . . . on a lot yet in view of the
decision of the author whoever he is to write about it
and the decision of yours truly to speak about it I should
like to invite those who are not put off by the hazards
of thought or the difficulties of language to take part in
what can only be called a game without necessarily
having to see them the way I do I don't actually say to
doubt them but extend to them the utmost efficacity of
the above-mentioned language. [*Pause. He turns back
to the desk, consults the text, etc. Faces the audience. Very
histrionic.*] It is not a question, gentlemen, of putting
spokes in the wheels of your understanding but of
preparing your faculties by an exposition of the obstacles
necessarily and as if deliberately proposed, by the path
we have to follow to arm themselves with patience and
lucidity. [*Consults text. etc.*] In the hypothesis of accept-
ance the question could not be posed more than once
the die would be cast and I should find myself if not
disposed at least obliged the word discomposes me but
pray understand me to suppose that which in the mind
of the presupposed author would seem if not to have
caused then at least to have caused to come to fruition
the idea of a deposition which is precisely what would
have been imposed on us by the hypothesis . . . [*Consults
text, etc.*] the hypothesis according to which he would
have been to a greater or lesser degree involved in the
events reposing at the basis of the whole edifice having
to be in the blinding light being in danger of over-
exposing the image I insist alas on the need for restraint

without prejudice for everyone whatsoever with the exception of those [*The projected image reappears twice as large as before. It is behind Mortin, who does not see it.*] who if they were not constantly reminded would let themselves be taken in and not because they were not warned taking into account the difficulties interposed and under this responsibility mine as witness the signature to the events exposed without any memorandum laboriously superimposed. [*He rubs his hands together with satisfaction, turning towards the bookshelves. He sees the image and starts back. It disappears. He brushes his hand over his eyes. Pause. Shrugs. Picks up his text from the desk and goes over to the bookshelves. Speaking normally*] The author the author where's the author . . . [*Glances mechanically at the titles of various books. Gesture of helplessness. Pause. Consults text, etc.*] There would be the real author or the one who out of the circumstance of the well would have constructed a hypothesis the supposed author being he who for however brief a time would have gone away with the manuscript and thrown it down the well . . . [*Consults text, etc.*] which author cannot be said to be related by the real one for how could the latter be called the real author when he is the one who puts forward the hypothesis that presupposes the manuscript, moreover the facts reported in the said manuscript how could the real author know about them without the existence of the supposed author the manuscript having gone down the drain in the well thus precluding not only the knowledge of the said facts but even that of their transcriber, and who could speak of the manuscript it would only be at the bottom of the well as the result of a hypothesis whence the doubly hypothetical nature of the authors they would not exist which would render inexplicable not only the possibility of a hypothesis but also that of any knowledge even a rough one of the facts recorded, who would know about them, who would have assembled them, who would have destroyed them, who would have found them again, who who who? [*Pause. He goes back to the table.*] As we were saying it would seem desirable to imagine some collusion between the real and the supposed authors . . . [*He pours himself out a glass of water and drinks it. Pause*] desire which would seem to imply their coexistence which would seem to be problematical . . . [*Pause*] In order to avoid this new danger might one not simply suppose this with all the usual reservations the possibility of the facts existing independently both of the authors and of the actors themselves . . . [*Consults text, etc., and turns towards the wall, still continuing his speech.*] the knowledge of which might be accessible to I won't say Tom Dick or Harry but to anyone endowed with a strong sense of identity, the question of who had knowledge of the facts and if they were real would then be minimised the said facts manifesting themselves so to speak outside their own eventuality . . . [*The image reappears twice as big as the last time. Mortin takes his glasses out of the inside pocket of his jacket, looks at them from a distance to see if they are clean, polishes them with his handkerchief and puts them on. Pause. The image moves its lips as if speaking. Pause. Mortin walks unhurriedly to the desk, goes round it, opens the drawer, takes out a revolver and checks the mechanism. Pause. He aims at the image and fires. Loud report. The face disappears. Mortin takes a duster out of the drawer, calmly wipes the revolver and puts it back in the drawer. Then goes over to the wall, examines the place where the bullet went in, and comes back to the desk. Sits down, puts glasses back in pocket, consults text, etc.*] the said facts manifesting themselves so to speak outside their own eventuality and taking hold of the person as any somewhat dense atmosphere might penetrating it and forcing it in spite of itself to give out a reflection of their false manifestness to which it would give a form that although assumed would none the less have all the appearances of being real. [*Pause*] The author then at his desk writing whether in draft or directly into the manuscript glued to the desk or on an original of which the manuscript glued to the desk would be only a replica or perhaps rather duplicate a question which for the moment I should call insoluble although it should not be in a setting that one might imagine almost similar to this [*Circular gesture*] not to get bogged down in too much detail a sparsely furnished room on the right bookshelves at the back a small stove standing out against a dazzling white wall to the left a table and an armchair where the author would be sitting writing writing writing what there would be the question difficult to insert a new hypothesis here it being certain that the manuscript thrown down the well could never have come to the knowledge of the author . . . come to the knowledge of the real author whom we should not attempt to identify because . . . [*Consults text. Angrily crosses out something he finds in it. Re-reads under his breath. Pause*] The author then sitting at his desk writing in the above-mentioned setting according to those who had more than a nodding acquaintance with him for without their valuable information what should we know let us be logical of the habits of the recluse and what should we know about these people themselves, neighbours? relations? a daughter? [*He gets up and walks about the room holding the text in his hand.*] No reason for excluding a priori the natural daughter. The advantage of this hypothesis would be a continuous presence a long acquaintance with the father's habits a real mine of information even if one thinks of the daughter shut away being freed in about say in about her forties from an unnatural father by sudden death, condemned all her life to the most degrading silence and suddenly restored to light and life on the day of the funeral, but extremely shy at first and only speaking to utter monosyllables like sod cracked brute shit . . . [*Pause. Consults text, etc.*] then gradually restored to confidence by the let us say neighbours and revealing all about her horrible life, getting up before daylight, emptying the rubbish, cleaning the privy, doing the washing-up from the day before or even the day before that so weak would she have felt the day before because of the privations perhaps even tortures, preparing a squalid meal of cabbage stumps and sour milk going to wake her father sleeping curled up on a pallet of straw being abused when she drew the curtain to let in a bit of light suggesting meekly that he might help her which would make the old man jump up and start beating her, going back to the kitchen and crying until her torturer starts up again and begins to guzzle up his skilly making a disgusting row slobbering spitting

the stumps in the wretched daughter's face then grab-
bing the old patched table-cloth to wipe his mouth
upsetting the soup-tureen and everything getting up
and rushing round the room whirling his arms about
[*Whirls his arms about. Pause*] whirling his arms about
. . . [*Consults text, etc.*] and hitting the wretched girl the
kitchen is so small stopping dead in the middle of the
room and relieving himself just to shock her and give
her still more work to do, going off shouting and leaving
his victim in the midst of his cabbage stumps and urine
and she in order not to waste a moment would start to
do the housework forgetting even to eat in spite of her
hunger her skirt dropping off her every so often so thin
would she be growing scouring in corners doing the
washing in cold water the tyrant's pants her own little
knickers all darned sometimes lifting her head up from
her work and starting to curse the day she was or wasn't
born asking herself questions without answers about
her mother repeating over and over again in her poor
little head the same two or three disconnected phrases . . .
[*Consults text, etc.*] disconnected phrases she'd have
heard her father say then back to work collapsing exhausted on to a stool and remaining prostrate for
hours without even the comfort of being able to read
or knit listening to the occasional sounds from outside
not daring to show her face at the window which anyway
would have been blocked up nor to go out into the little
courtyard where anyway you couldn't have moved for
all the heaps of furniture in various styles second-hand
stuff belonging to one of the tenants who didn't consider anyone else's convenience waiting for the happy

night when the tyrant wouldn't call her twenty times running to pick up the revolting pellet he would always be picking out of his nose and rolling between his fingers and throwing on the floor sometimes making his victim swallow it without blenching the least sign of disgust on her part bringing down a volley of blows and kicks all this for forty years until the blessed day of the death and the funeral. [*Pause. He goes and sits down and drinks a glass of water. Takes out his handkerchief and mops his brow. Puts handkerchief back in his pocket. Wets his finger and counts the number of pages still left to recite. Pause.*] Stick it, gentlemen, stick it. One can well imagine the poor girl one morning going to her father's room and finding him lying crooked his head hanging out of bed his eyes fixed and his mouth open at first she'd think it was a trick the old man was always one for play-acting, she'd stand in the doorway expecting to be subjected to the usual sarcasm or rain of insults waiting a while then making up her mind to speak. Dad it's time to get up, saying it again after a couple of minutes and then again louder then cautiously approaching the body, suddenly forcing back a cry at the sight of death her instinct telling her that such was the cᴀ⸱ ⸴ since even a creature utterly devoid of judgᵣₑₙₜ . . . devoid of judgment . . . would soon ᵣⸯ⸴ₐ to that sort of evidence standing rooted to the spot and unconsciously mimicking the dead man then suddenly running to the window [*He suddenly gets up and goes through the motions of opening a window on to the audience*] and opening it to the street and calling out ow ow ow like the animal she would be so that a woman passing would turn round and a window opposite open, going on shrieking and rousing everyone and soon breaking into nervous sobs impossible to say whether of laughter or terror staying at the window nearly ten minutes until one of the people in the crowd by now gathered below would realize there must have been an accident and entering the house would force his way into the room and call for help the poor woman having begun to throw her arms about and roll on the floor holds her down and with the help of a kind bystander brings her out into the street and gives her into the charge of some women at the sight of whom the unfortunate creature calms down. [*Pause. He picks the text up off the table again and goes over to the bookshelves. Turns towards the audience. An image twice the size of the previous one appears on the wall. Mortin, who does not see it, continues his recitation.*] Only after many days thanks to the care bestowed by the charitable souls . . . [*Pause. Consults text, etc.*] who would take it in turns to watch by her bedside the sick woman for that's what she'd be would begin to cease vomiting which she'd have been doing till then because of the shrinking of her stomach which would not be able to cope with the rich food they would have forced her to wallow so blind is the solicitude of those determined to be helpful and to speak the few monosyllables previously quoted which first of all would scandalize the females but they would soon get used to it in their eagerness to know more about her and the unnatural father who'd kept her shut up then she'd start to quieten down and weaken till she'd be in a sort of prostration [*The image speaks, but the words cannot be distinguished. They make a murmur that gradually increases in volume until the end of Mortin's sentence, at which point he notices it.*] that would last several days the doctor having come meanwhile and prescribed drip-feeding . . . drip-feeding but showing no serious anxiety and making everyone wait patiently until the day when indeed the invalid regaining strength would begin in her con-valescence not without great difficulty at first to talk of her beast of burden's life not addressing her interlocutors so to speak but as if talking to herself the former all interpreting her monologue in their own ways and these interpretations eventually reaching the rest of the world in garbled versions so that to uncleanness would be added immorality to immorality bestiality to bestiality the supernatural not one of these interpretations being worthy of credence to a decently balanced mind. [*Pause. He turns round at the noise now issuing from the image. Remains very calm and listens to it rattling on with his back to the audience.*]

IMAGE OF MORTIN: . . . Same continuous presence same long acquaintance with the father's habits real mine of exactly opposite information if one only thinks of an affectionate girl deprived in about say in her thirties of the love of an adored father through natural causes used to the most delicate care and the most refined conversation and suddenly thrust upon brutal reality the day of the funeral extremely low-spirited at first and never ceasing to utter laments mingled with endear-ments like darling kitten pet angel, etc., then through her tears revealing to the let us say neighbours the delights of her former existence woken up at noon by father who would have already emptied the rubbish cleaned the privy done the washing-up for that day and the day after so anxious would he have been to help her given breakfast in bed by the kind old gentleman who'd cram her first with sweets and vitamins then leave her to doze till lunch-time and go and prepare a meal of turtle-doves and rabbit stuffed with sweet almonds coming to wake her again not liking to draw the muslin curtain for fear of waking her whispering softly in her ear that she must wake up and still not waking her going back to the kitchen and humming lullabies until the spoiled darling would deign to declare herself awake and come and sit dreamily at the table and knock back her lunch [*Mortin puts his head in his hands. Back still to the audience.*] washing it down with Spanish wine chatting pleasantly the while wiping the corner of her mouth from time to time with a handkerchief of Venetian lace and fascinating her father by the plumpness and grace of her whole person so that he would get up and plant a chaste kiss on his child's brow a kiss both chaste and passionate then restraining his transports he would start to recite a long poem about nothing else but her charms at last managing to tear himself away would go back to his study still humming leaving her to belch at leisure over her coffee of which she wouldn't be able to make up her mind whether to have a second cup divided between the desire to go back to sleep and that of reaching out for the coffee-pot pondering long over the dilemma then finally going back to sleep and dreaming of her little mama who came from an aristocratic family and reciting to her by way of compliment papa's poem embellishing it with her own little philological and lexicographical discoveries turning it in her innocence into a veritable masterpiece of spun-sugar stupidity hearing through the veils of half-sleep the sound of a limousine passing in the avenue or the nice little boy on the fifth floor whistling like a lark in courtyard waking up again at last at dusk and going to give papa a surprise taking him a chocolate truffle out of the sideboard and saying shut your eyes and open your mouth and all this for thirty years until the evil day of the death and the funeral. [*The image disappears. Mortin turns towards the bookshelves. Sudden attack of rage. He takes hold of the books one by one and throws them about the room. Then goes and sits down and drinks a glass of water. Pause. Consults text, lifts head and continues articulating his speech, at first without making any s und. Twenty seconds of this, then normal voice.*]

MORTIN: It would be best in order not to get bogged down in unnecessary detail which is in any case unknown about the way the recluse spent his days to tackle the episode of the going away in the middle of he night which we have suggested was a critical one in t e history of the manuscript. Let us imagine the author or evening the mind worn out by long unsystematic labou suddenly realizing the futility of all his effort and fall ng into a dejection which would manifest i. ˙ ˡᶠ phys ally by a relaxation of all the muscles resulting in a su len alteration in his facial appearance and all his ody even internally and causing a descent if not of tl digestive organs at least of their products . . . [*Consults text. Laughs. Takes glasses out of his pocket, puts hem on and looks more closely. Loud guffaw. Goes on read ng under his breath, turns over the page. Puts glasses back n his pocket. Looks up.*] So there is our hero buried up t the armpits and what little energy remains to him thus diminished on the point of perishing in the midst of this untoward defecation. It should be noted in passing that the best part of all our energy and will-power probably resides in these substances and if our loss of them should be too copious . . . if our loss of them should be too copious . . . we should enter the same condition of complete prostration as the author was in that evening. If we were all professional humanists we should fiercely oppose all products causing the evacuation of what we might without exaggeration call our specific being. [*Pause*] Indeed how can one resist dreaming of the day when the human race will be awake at last to a true consciousness of itself restored by an enlightened constipation, emulation between human beings forgotten every man sure of becoming the equal of the great by means of a sustained asceticism, a new hope, a complete reappraisal of values, philosophy and religion establishing themselves on solid bases, the scales falling from our eyes and God himself appearing to humanity at last in the form of an enormous heap of . . . [*Consults text. Idiotic laugh. Pause. Looks up.*] As we were saying his mind worn out with long unsystematic labour. Indeed that would be the most likely hypothesis for explaining the decision he would make at that crucial moment unless we are to suppose that having a presentiment of his approaching end and not having been able to complete the work whose logic was equalled only by its solidity he decides through some scruple to put it out of the reach of the public's curiosity by throwing it down the well making the ultimate concession to his vanity as a writer by not consigning it to the flames of his stove.

[*Pause*] Why concession, because to a man with a mind so profoundly imbued with love of his work immersion . . . [*Consults text, etc.*] would appear less irrevocable as a means of destruction allowing the possibility of a providential fishing up again though he didn't permit himself to think of that happening even in the most distant future. [*Pause*] Why so profoundly imbued with love of his work, because in the conditions of our hypothesis . . . [*Consults text. The image appears, double its previous size. Mortin pays no attention to it, re-reading his text under his breath while the image answers the questions posed.*]

IMAGE OF MORTIN: Because in the conditions of our hypothesis it would seem to us more appealing that the author should be presented from the point of view of this vulnerability since this would facilitate belief in the rest of the hypothesis or its corollaries.

MORTIN: *reading*] Why should the presentation of the author from the point of view of this vulnerability facilitate belief in the rest of the hypothesis . . . [*A second image appears beside the first. They answer in unison. Mortin buries his nose in the text.*]

IMAGES OF MORTIN: Because the emotional element added to the author's character by presenting him from this point of view would make our inquiry seem more human by making him seem somehow less gratuitous you catch more flies with honey than with vinegar and the slightest reference to some sentimental weakness in a person automatically awakens interest in him in the minds of the curious if you want proof take the fabulous amount of much relating to the love lives of perfect strangers the papers regale us with these days with the sole object of increasing their sales.

MORTIN: *reading*] Why having a presentiment of his approaching end . . . [*A third image appears. As before*]

IMAGES OF MORTIN: Because in view of the isolation in which we suppose our author would live not to go into the question of his age which we don't know in view of his inability to share his feelings which would thereby have grown atrophied and tough in view moreover of the difficulties he would have come up against in his work and which would remain inexplicably unsurmounted in spite of all his efforts difficulties moreover which he would mistakenly regard as inseparable from the pursuit of a literary ideal [*Mortin stops his ears*] but which are really to be regarded as part and parcel of his moral or physical nature paradox being its most common manifestation as to laugh instead of weep or to belch instead of fart this latent despair increasing to the point where it would blot out the future entirely for him it would seem plausible to suppose that a revelation should declare itself in him concerning his last end since it seems that a certain inaptitude to assume the impedimenta of existence would indicate a congenital weakness the cause of which or vice versa it would not be incorrect to ascribe to a total disbelief in the aforesaid existence a lack which would show itself in the above-mentioned presentiment which moreover might well have been manifest from the tenderest youth and continue until say ninety why put it out of reach of the curiosity of the public because the idea of leaving behind him either a heap of inextricable ineptitudes or work unfinished [*Mortin seizes his manuscript, jumps up and goes and throws it into the stove. He then remains standing in the middle of the room, stopping his ears, facing the audience. The images speak faster and faster, louder and louder. Fierce expression.*] the rigour of which could not admit its being left incomplete would be intolerable to his vanity as an author which while it might be regarded by the profane as no less vain than ridiculous would find justification in the fact that a man who has not as they say lived and has taken refuge entirely in his work might well set his heart on appearing to posterity in a light of his own choosing a flattering light admitting of no variation since the smallest wavering might distort his chosen visage which he would rather see annihilated for ever than imperfect it being possible for this fabrication to equal the breathing sweating copulating human creature which he never was only on condition that it was exactly as he wished it to be why condition because profession why profession because destruction why destruction because prevision why because why because why because why because why because why because why because why because why because . . .

[*The images disappear. Pause. Mortin lets his hands fall. Very long pause. Then he suddenly takes off his jacket and throws it behind him. Then his tie. Then his shirt. Then his trousers. Can't decide whether to take off his underpants. Keeps them on. Takes off his shoes and socks. Stands motionless for a while. Goes over and sits in the chair. Pause. Gets up ⌐ . goes back into the middle of the room. Pause. Speaˡ ⌐a a hesitating, broken voice.*]

MORTIN: In the end he'd go . . . [*Pause*] He'ˡ put his manuscript under his arm . . . shut the door . . . go . . . in the middle of the night . . . to the well . . . [*Pause*] He'd cross the little path all choked with nettles . . . catch his foot in a wire . . . fall down . . . get up again. . . . still holding on to the manuscript . . . [*Pause*] He'd come out on to the little road with acacias planted along it and those evil-smelling plants what do they call them . . . what do they call them . . . [*Pause*] He'd keep on towards the well which would be . . . more than ever in his heart . . . necessary . . . to the failure that was his life . . . [*Pause*] As he walked he'd say to himself . . . recite . . . a speech . . . a speech on the wreckage . . . the wreckage . . . in which other solitaries like him would have tried all their lives . . . to give a meaning to death . . . a meaning to death . . . without even knowing . . . that that was what it was all about . . . through all the little changes and chances of their lives . . . [*Pause*] A trite speech . . . which he'd suddenly realize . . . [*Pause*] a trite speech which he'd recognize as being the one in the manuscript under his arm . . . [*Pause*] And he'd be quite astonished . . . he'd never have suspected . . . to find that he'd been making symbols . . . [*Pause*] He'd find in the foolish last words . . . the key to the complicated dreams . . . that he would have liked to express so brilliantly in his book . . . [*Pause*] He wouldn't regret anything . . . not any more . . . because he'd have put his finger at last . . . on his real trouble . . . [*Pause*] There would go through his mind . . . through his mind . . . all the missed opportunities to be silent . . . [*Pause*] They'd seem to him too late the only ones . . . too late the only ones . . . that ever had a chance . . . of solving the mystery . . . the mystery . . . [*Pause*] The missed opportunities to be silent . . . [*Pause*] The missed opportunities . . .

CURTAIN

DATE DUE

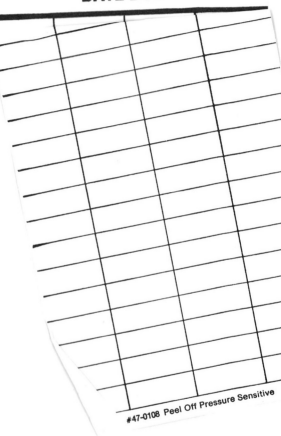

#47-0108 Peel Off Pressure Sensitive